Step

Contents

Acknowledgements

Writing a book is an extensive process that indebts a person to more people than one can ever repay. Nevertheless, I need to give a special thanks to my loving wife Gina who has painstakingly read this manuscript more times than I can count, and also provided both constructive criticism and loving support. Likewise, my best friend Ron Chicken has endured many multi-hour discussions with me on weighty topics. This text would not have been worth reading if it had not been for his sharp mind.

I also need to recognize Dr. James Stacy Taylor, who's systematic philosophical instruction equipped me to undertake such a project, Dr. Roy A. Clouser, who's tireless dedication to intellectually rigorous Christianity inspired me to do so, and Reverend Richard Kocses, whose extensive theological instruction fills this volume. The present work has also benefited from my research at Princeton Theological Seminary with its ample resources covering Dutch

Neo-Calvinism and Scottish Common Sense Philosophy. This would not have been possible without the tireless work of Gordon Graham. And Likewise, Dean Zimmerman kindly including me in the Rutgers's philosophy of religion reading group and gave me important critical feedback.

Furthermore, *Who Is God?* would not be what it is today without the generous editing work of Diana Sand and the cover art of Dalton Ackerman. Finally, this work is indebted to the kind graces of Sister Josephine Aparo and Frank and Ruth Beitz for their willingness to freely give me a roof over my head when I needed it; and to Mr. Huff for granting me a full tuition scholarship. Without these people's help I never would have completed my theological education.

Chapter 1 – Who is God?

Paul picked himself up off the cold concrete and stumbled away from Blue's Night Club in a blurry daze. His head pounded as he spat out blood. What a shame. After all, the night had started off looking so good.

When he first arrived, the club was packed with more scantily clad gorgeous women than a Victoria's Secret catalogue. Strippers were dancing in cages suspended from the ceiling while the open bar kept pouring out the good times. Pounding beats mixed with gyrating bodies creating one carnal motion. Paul surveyed the dance floor filled with intertwined people and smelled sweat mingled with lust. He felt a surge of satisfaction. The hunting grounds were littered with prey and tonight the game was on!

Paul's young, athletic frame and bold features always turned heads when he entered a room. A long work week had left him bored out of his mind and in need to blow off steam. He was disappointed that both of his wing men were out of action and almost called the party off. But he was glad he hadn't when a shapely blond with a dress that left little to the imagination eyed him up. He easily slid next to her and ordered two drinks. She smiled, and Paul knew he'd hit the mark.

Paul later scored with this blond, a brunette, and a Latina before the ecstasy. Normally he would never go for something harder than a drink when flying solo. But somewhere between Mary (or was it Maria?) and Trish, Paul decided to ride his wave of luck. The whole world started to glow as another hot babe ran her fingers up and down his body. Every whiff of her scent and caress of her touch plunged him into an explosion of sensations.

A little after two in the morning, Paul tried to reel in a sleek fiery red head with the eyes of a virgin and the moves of a pole dancer. As the music commanded the throng to become animals, Paul advanced with his signature move. First, he eyed up the dancing girl with a stoic glance revealing nothing but mystery. He slid his body close to hers. Leading her eyes down the length of his frame with the smooth motion of his hands, he baited her in, playing her hips like a medicine man on drums. Then he added her lips to his list of instruments. But the next thing he knew a bellowing man with bloodshot eyes came charging across the dance floor.

"HEY YOU! GET OFF MY GIRL!" Paul turned just in time to see the massive behemoth's swing. The man's punch crushed Paul's face and knocked him off both his game and his feet in one fell motion. He felt like porcelain shattering under the weight of a sledge hammer. Within seconds the dance floor became a fighting ring for the two combatants. Paul tried to get his bearings even though the drugs and sudden pounding left him struggling to keep the room from spinning. He took a weak swing at the enraged lover, but only struck air. Before Paul knew what was happening the attacker brought a heavy heel down onto his gut and landed on top of him.

Paul had spent enough years in the martial arts to know he could never return punches while flat on his back. He reached up and dug both his thumbs into the attacker's eyes. The man's scream pierced Paul's ears as he shifted his weight and threw the attacker onto the floor. Reverberations ran up Paul's arm as he landed his first solid punch. The crowd cheered as the man's nose fractured and blood splattered across the floor. Paul would have beaten him into submission, but the bouncers moved in first. They tore Paul off and dragged him to the door as colors and screaming faces rushed by.

Paul mumbled "Gerroff me....I didn' do anyfing!"

"Shut up!" the bouncers screamed as they tossed him outside and slammed the club's back door. He could still hear the crowd cheering behind him...there's nothing quite like violence to spice up sex. Paul laid face down on cold concrete in the back alley behind the club. His head spun as the warm blood gushing down his face told him his nose was broken.

Alone in the dark alleyway, Paul shivered as the cold concrete wrenched the heat from his feverish skin. The bruises swelling across his body felt like they would burst. His quickening headache felt like a jackhammer pounding the back of his skull in sync with the music still pouring through the door behind him. Even shifting his weight felt like a struggle against the oppressive chains of gravity. Eventually Paul found the strength to force himself to his knees and then to his feet. He concentrated on moving one leg at a time until he reached a wall to lean against and pulled out his phone. Its screen had shattered somewhere amidst the scuffle. "Oh damn," muttered Paul as he cast it aside. Exhausted, he looked up into the night sky, and yelled, "Whad are you doin' to me?"

Thoughts crawled across his consciousness with as much grace as his feet across the ally. *No phone...oh God, it hurts...damn Ecstasy...gotta shake this...gotta get home...walk it off, just walk it off.* He meandered forward, his swagger replaced by the strained motions of a beaten man, slowly searching for the red light district's main street. Sooner or later, the poison would wear away and his head would be clear enough to get him home...hopefully.

Paul stumbled for what felt like hours, passing by the other joints in the city's cesspool of sin. There were dance clubs, gay clubs, sports bars, strip bars, and pretty much every other type of venue that someone seeking quick pleasure could ask for. Neon signs shouted, "Girls! Girls! Girls!", "Happy Hour Every Hour", and "Safari Night! Black Girls Galore". Paul was bombarded by clashing waves of music and a flood of changing lights emanating from every nightclub.

Paul tripped over the curb and stumbled into a

couple gay guys going at it on a street corner. "Hey, get outta here you...!" Well, the rest of the words were more colorful than his skimpy neon yellow short shorts with rainbow trim. The other shoved him into a nearby trashcan and Paul toppled over. He lay covered in filth, too exhausted to move as pain surged through his body.

Paul clutched the back of his head before feeling his face. He knew he was in bad shape and needed to find help, but didn't want to move yet. Amid heavy breathing the young man began scanning his surroundings. A grizzled man with a trench coat and half fingered gloves stood over to the far right. He eyed Paul up with dark curiosity. To the left, an older man in a suit disappeared into a dark alley with his arm around a young teenage girl in a miniskirt and hooker boots. A sharp, cold breeze rustled down the city streets blowing trash about. The distant sound of a couple several stories above him screaming at each other while a baby cried in the background echoed across the cityscape.

Paul's mind began to race. *Where...what...where is this? Middle of a street... middle of a dark street... covered in trash ... nose is bleeding ... somebody gonna mug me ... or somebody gonna rape me?* Paul noticed the grizzled man in the trench coat pulling something out of his pocket. He was still eyeing Paul up head to toe with a twisted joker grin that was growing wider. A single clear thought ran through the young man's foggy mind:

Run!

Paul bolted to his feet and sprinted as fast as an injured man could. He never looked back, more out of fear then a conscious decision. People parted and spat insults as he flew past them. There were more old men disappearing into van's or back allies with young girls, people shivering by fires burning in trashcans, offensive odors from accumulated filth, and the eclectic mix of sensual sounds and bickering, all of which passed into a blur. Finally, Paul could endure no more. He came to a stop and heaved great gulps of air. Frantically, he searched for the shady man in the trench coat but found no sign of him. Still, Paul decided it was safer to keep moving.

Normally when Paul walked down these streets at night some girls would openly ask if he was looking for a good time. Although the honest answer was yes, he would always ignore them. The forward girls were

the ones you had to pay for, which was never worth
the money since so many free ones were available for
guys like Paul. Besides, you never knew what you
might catch from a call girl. Oh, and if you were
desperate enough to pay for sex than you had to be
pretty raunchy yourself, which meant you had to be
passing on something pretty raunchy to whatever girl
you were paying.

Not to mention that in this part of town you
never knew if the person was really a woman. A buddy
of Paul's had once paid for a girl and had to run when
"she" turned out to be a "he". Still, Paul liked call girls
since they were more pretty faces trying to flirt with
him. Right now though, no one was looking at him
unless they were staring in disgust or laughing. Who
could blame them? Paul knew he was covered in
blood, but there was little he could do besides wipe his
face with his sleeve and keep moving.

Eventually Paul wandered far enough to hear a
voice that clashed with the rest of this place.
Everything here was designed to make you forget
about the real world. Drugs, sex, music…it was all
there to make you think about the moment and never
a second longer. But there was one standard fixture

here that always nagged at the back of your mind; the crazy preacher who stood near the entrance of the red light district where the music was just quiet enough to hear him. Paul, and everybody else, knew that this guy had absolutely no life. In fact, he was anti-life. Most people who never work up the courage to go out and have a good time at least leave the others who do alone. They live and let live. But this guy seemed to thrive on crushing the joy of everyone around him. His mere presence could make you feel shameful, angry, or both.

Under different circumstances Paul would have turned around and walked away. The last thing his ringing ears needed was a hell fire sermon. But right now he needed some protection and a strange idea took root in his mind.

Easy target...too easy...gotta get safe...trench coat guy is still out there...no bull by a preacher. So Paul hobbled through party heaven until he reached the nearest bench to the evangelist. He thought the man's voice sounded like the foul offspring of a Puritan and a lawn mower. It was loud, obnoxious, and carried well, but kept making the same noise.

"There is something missing from all our lives.

We try to fill it anyway we can. Some search for money, others sex, still others want power, or perhaps entertainment. Here in a region blessed by economic prosperity it is extremely easy to lose oneself in an endless stream of entertainment. We have redirected the resources of the land into a hedonistic search for pleasure. But this pleasure never satisfies for more than a moment. As soon as the high ends, another is wanted. As soon as the surge of adrenaline fades, a new excitement is sought. Well, many years ago a man told a woman who was living just such a life, a life that had led her to lie with many men and now live with another who was not her husband, that He knew what could satisfy her. This man claimed that He was living water, and that whoever drank of that living water would never thirst again. This man was Jesus, and if you would only drink of this water, you too could receive His satisfying grace, and come to know the living God who can sustain you and fill you in a way that all the earthly pleasures never will!"

Another young twenty-something walking past with a group of guys called out, "So Jesus wanted to SATISFY her? Well, okay, I'm gonna head over to one of those strip joints and pull a Jesus by tapping a

Mary, but she won't be a virgin by the time I'm done!" His friends and everyone else within ear shot laughed and scoffed. The preacher, however, seemed undaunted. He continued on, "For God so loved the world that he gave his only begotten son, that whosoever might believe in him would have eternal life." The young man called out again, "And I'll keep lovin' to satisfy the lives of all the ladies God put here with devilish deeds." Now the preacher was silent. He waited until the young man, his posse, and their snide comments trailed off in the distance.

Paul took a long look at the preacher. He had passed by the man at least a dozen times and always laughed or cringed, depending on whether or not anyone nearby had recently made a joke at the man's expense, but never really looked hard at him before. He was older, maybe in his late fifties or early sixties. His hair was graying and his skin was covered in lines. He wore a tweed jacket and held a black, leather-bound King James Bible in his hand. The binding was well worn and the corners were frayed. Everything about this aging, conservatively dressed grandfather figure belching Bible verses from the 17th century clashed with the district around him. Once Paul had heard him talking about some poem, or song, or something like that in the Bible written by Solomon...or was it Saul...whichever was the wise one... and how much he loved this woman. Paul thought he remembered another time when he preached out of Proverbs 23 (or was it 24?) about the Lord being a shepherd, and how we should not want, for the Lord's rod and staff would comfort us.

Paul actually felt sympathy for the man. This guy was nearing the end of his life with apparently nothing to live for. Every Friday and Saturday night he would come out here, sometimes like tonight he would even be all alone, and preach to a bunch of young college and early career clubbers in their prime. No one wanted to hear a word he had to say, and yet he kept talking. What could have possibly gone wrong in his life to make him stand out on a street corner twice a week and be ignored or berated? Every once in a while someone would start an argument with him or spit at him. Some said that once, several years back, a guy had even punched him in the face and run off. Yet, the old man persisted.

Whatever sympathy Paul had for the preacher quickly evaporated when the preacher began walking towards him. Paul already regretted his decision to come here. *Damn it, why? Run? Hide? Crap, too late! I...*

"My goodness! Sir, are you alright?" Paul stared blankly at the man, trying to register his question. "You stay right there, I'm going to get you some help." He quickly darted off to the nearest business, which happened to be the Hell Fire Go Go Bar (so named for its red light theme and the naughty devil costumes of the waitresses). *Does he preach here just for the irony?* Paul thought. A couple minutes later the preacher emerged from Hell with a damp wash cloth, a pink rimmed mirror, and a couple water bottles. He sat next to Paul and handed him the cloth and mirror. "Let me know when you're done with the mirror, I promised one of the girls I would get it back to her." Paul shuddered. Something about the thought of a preacher going into the Hell Fire Go Go Bar to ask a stripper for a favor, all with pious intentions, didn't sit well with him.

Paul reluctantly took both items and began to clean his face. He looked like a disaster. Thankfully the bleeding had stopped, but it had left behind a caked river of dark red next to numerous bruises and

a black eye. Paul was hoping the preacher wouldn't
strike up a conversation, but all his former good luck
had run out. "You know, I've been preaching on this
street corner for over ten years and that's the first time
I ever spent money in one of these places. Well, I guess
there's a first time for everything." Paul's raised
eyebrows told the evangelist how strange that
sounded. The preacher smiled as he continued, "Well
that wasn't much. I actually know the bar tender
there. Good guy, not that I like his chosen vocation,
but I use to coach his son in little league. Real talented
family." Paul hated the awkward silence that followed,
but at least it was better than trying to make sense out
of the preacher innocently chatting with bar tenders
and scantily clad woman. Unfortunately, all good
things come to an end.

"So...are you okay? I mean, it looks like you
really took a beating. Would you like to go to the
hospital? I can make a call and..."

"No."

"Um... are you sure?"

"Yeah...thanks."

Another long silence passed, but the preacher
seemed oblivious to the awkwardness. Paul downed

both the water bottles over the next ten minutes or so hoping to lessen the hangover in the morning. Finally the preacher spoke again stretching out his hand, "Oh wow! Where are my manners? My name is Moses, but you can call me Mo. And you are?"

Moses...who...Moses? Probably homeschooled from some back woods, hick trailer park. Still, nice guy. Paul reluctantly shook the man's hand and mumbled, "Paul".

And then the preaching began. "Well Paul, nice name by the way. I've got the question of a lifetime for you: do you know who God is? Are you ready to receive the Grace of God?" Now on a good day, metaphysical meanderings usually struck Paul as a waste of time. He remembered his freshmen year in college taking a philosophy class. The experience only affirmed his inclination that if there is a God somewhere out there, we will never know who He is in this life. The only thing that waste of time had accomplished was placating Paul's pushy, born again, older brother.

"No."

Mo smiled, grinning ear to ear. Paul could picture what must be going through the man's mind as his victim lay helplessly caught within a web. Day in and day out the evangelist searched for that one sucker who he could ensnare in his trap and steal fifty minutes of the sitting duck's time while only paying out a pamphlet and a headache in return. Paul was unable to get away easily given his state of mind. He could not tell the old man to get lost after all the guy had just done for him, and was too strung out to say much. Now the preacher could give his whole why-Jesus-loves-you song and dance and there was nothing Paul could do but endure it. *Well, better this then trench coat guy. Maybe...*

"Well Paul, God is the composite of everything good and noble. He is the greatest and most desirable thing we could ever strive for," said Mo while looking directly into Paul's eyes. Paul knew where this was going, and despite the man's kindness, he wanted to spare himself the coming agony.

Paul directed all his energy into his words. "Look, dude...you're nice, okay. You got me water." He motioned to the bottle and washcloth before noticing the words on the back of the mirror, "Naughty Girls have all the Fun" scrawled next to its "Hell Fire" Logo. The thought of Mo chatting to one of those strippers sent weird shivers down his spine.

"Um...yeah...but I don't buy into any of this God stuff. I just need rest."

"Oh...Oh I see. I suppose this is a late hour to be out and about on such streets. Over the years I've seen some trouble in these parts. You know just a few months back there was a stabbing a couple blocks from here. I shudder to think how many rapes happen in these parts. Normally I come out here with some friends. It's safer that way. But, even by myself I'm usually okay as long as I stick to the main street. You just never want to get off the straight path, otherwise you can rear onto dangerous ground.

"Kind of like real life. You know, the Lord describes the way to heaven as a straight and narrow path, whereas the one that leads to destruction is broad and well-traveled. I know someone who 'doesn't buy into this God stuff' probably doesn't put much stock in these kinds of analogies, but seriously think about it. Why is it that in a place where Jesus is the farthest thing from everyone's mind, you need to keep an eye out for yourself? Might it be that the wisdom of God breeds the kindness of man, whereas a den of iniquity breeds foolishness?"

Despite his drugged daze Paul was becoming

enraged at all this God talk. The anger sharpened his senses enough to spit a few quick, semi-articulate sentences. "Look, God, He might be out there. Maybe somewhere on the other side of the universe is a big, barrel chested man with a lightning bolt. Maybe He's ready to smite bad people and reward good people. But from where I'm sitting..." Paul swung his arms out and gestured to his filthy surroundings, and almost fell off his seat. He quickly grabbed the bench and held it firmly before continuing.

"It looks like God, if there is a God, doesn't care too much about my life or what I'm doing. If religion works for you then cool, whatever makes you happy..." Paul again stopped. The pounding in his head had grown with his escalating temper. He clutched the side of his head until the veins in his hands bulged. Mo looked like he was about to speak until Paul cut him off. "But it's not for me. I got a ton of this stuff when I was growing up. My Dad...stupid old man...was OBESSESED with God. By the time I moved out, he was finishing another book about the Bible..."

There were too many heightened sensations. Everything felt exasperated by the drugs until the faintest sound or color dominated his mind. All Paul wanted to do was retreat into a nice, warm, soft, quiet, and dark place away from criminals, clubs, and most of all, preachers that could give you headaches at will. "Stupid old man finished another book every other week...quoted scripture like it was written on the back of his hand. But he was just a stupid old man – what did he know? Then my big brother came back from college all Christian and wanted me to read all these Jesus books too..." Now Paul was grinding his teeth between sentences. "I've seen your song and dance...it's not for me...take the sale's pitch and go look for somebody who's buying 'cause I'm not."

Mo kept looking into Paul the whole time. Those wide eyes seemed completely focused on what he was doing and stood totally unabated at the resistance they had just met. Compared to what they usually had to deal with, this must have been a vacation. "Well, it looks like you've had a rough night, and I certainly cannot make you accept Christ. Maybe we should change the topic. You know, talk about something that will distract you a bit. I'm really not trying to make things go from bad to worse. But first, I would like to challenge you to one day think again about who Jesus is and what He means for your life. Christ died in order to give you the most valuable thing that anyone of us can receive: the free gift of Grace whose loving kindness can make us whole again. Would you be willing to take this gospel of John, and when you get your head back on straight, read it? You have nothing to lose and eternity to gain." Paul had had enough. Something about the way this guy talked just made him feel all wrong. He was trying to sell something, and picking on a guy who's been beaten up and high is just not the right thing to do or the right time to do it.

Paul steadied himself against the bench and stood up. He began to back away off the curb and onto the street. "Thanks, but I don't know God and I don't want to know God. I can't know God and even if I could I still wouldn't. God, if He is out there, is a distant ghost. Maybe an equation or the whole universe, but not a person and definitely not some dead guy hanging on a tree. He certainly doesn't care about us. If He did, this whole world would be a very different place. All I know is that..."

The young man had tripped over his own feet as he backed into the street. The extra yard his tumble had taken put him in the path of oncoming traffic. Mo suddenly jumped off his bench and bolted towards him yelling Paul's name, but it was too late. As would come out in court some time later, the driver of the red mustang that smashed into him was too drunk to know when to stop. By the time Mo reached him, Paul was already broken and unconscious on the ground...

....

Mo's face looked as grave as a tombstone as he spoke with another man dressed in a white lab coat. "Yes doctor, he seemed pretty out of it when I was talking to him. His responses were very slow and short to start. But he became more alert after some time and water. By the end he was pretty excited and defensive. Do you know if he will live?"

"At this point it's too difficult to tell. It's tough to take that much trauma when your body is at its best, but this guy has a whole slew of poison in his system which is going to make everything, especially medicating him, more complicated. Right now we have done all that we can do."

"Has anyone come to see him?"

"His family has been notified but will not be arriving for a couple days."

"So he might die alone?! We can't have that. Do you mind if I stay with him. I would like to pray for him."

"Normally we do not allow non-family members that kind of access, but seeing that right now you're the only "family" he's got I think we can bend the rules. Besides, it would be good to keep someone in the room with him. Let us know if anything changes."

Paul lay on a hospital bed wrapped up like a mummy with tubes, liquids, and all kinds of monitoring machines around him. He had a vague awareness that people were talking about him, but that only lasted for a fleeting moment. Consciousness faded, and Paul was somewhere in between dreaming and another place.

Chapter 2 – God is a Dancer

Paul was back in the club, but it was empty. He walked back and forth, looking for some sign of life, yet found none. This was the same club he had been dancing in earlier that evening. The place was glowing with neon lights and swirling lasers, but without any people or sound besides the echoes of his footsteps, the whole scene seemed eerie. "Hell...Hello? Is anybody here?"

"Looking sharp stud," said a feminine voice from behind him. He quickly spun around. Even in the poor lighting Paul could see that the woman in front of him was absolutely stunning. With dark hair that went down to her shoulders, a slender blue dress that stopped midway down her thighs, and a body to match, Paul was more mesmerized by the way she walked towards him than by any drug he had ever tried. As she drew closer his eyes latched onto her exquisite necklace. It was made of three glass triangles cut to look like crystals bound in bronze casings, and strung together on interlocking, ornate, bronze chains. It glittered in the changing light.

He could make out the details of her face as she drew near. She seemed familiar, and when she finally stopped barely a forearm away, he had the strange feeling he had met her before. Maybe she was the second girl he had hooked up with that night? If so, then she had been a great dancer, one of the best he had seen. They had grinded for a while and eventually made out, but she excused herself before he really got to talk to her. By the time she came back, Paul was with a new girl and the opportunity was lost. On second thought, her dress looked more like one of the girls from last week. Oh well, eventually they all start to look the same.

"So, you want to know, right?"

Paul wrinkled his brow and stared into her eyes. "Do I want to know what?"

She smiled. "Do you want to know a secret?"

Paul wanted to ask a dozen questions. How did he get here? Why were all the other people gone? Why was his face fine, his head no longer throbbing, and his cloths clean? What was this woman doing here? Did she stay behind to try to find him? What on earth was that rose-scented perfume she was wearing? Was she single? If not, did that matter? What was her number? Oh yeah, and what was her name?

But half out of reflex and half out of instinct he decided to play along. "Baby I love secrets, especially ones from a beautiful woman like yourself."

She smiled and drew closer. "Well I can't just tell you, but I think I can show you."

Oh? This one seems as fun as she looks, Paul thought with a sly smile. "Okay, I'm listening...and watching," as he eyed her up from head to toe.

The woman raised her hands over her head and clapped. With that the music started playing. She leaned forward and pressed her pointer finger over his mouth while moving her own lips close to his ear.

She whispered, "You talk too much. You don't need to do that right now. Just listen, and dance." She placed his hands around her waist, and the two began to sway.

Paul was too impressed to know how to respond to this beautiful stranger. Everything about her was intoxicating, from the way she would effortlessly glide up and down the floor to how she just lost herself in the neon lights and music. There was something different about her. Most of the time when he danced with girls he felt like he was playing chess, only in this game the goal was to take the queen. He had many times approached a girl with a stoic expression, glanced up and down her, and then with one smooth motion come next to her and begun to jive with the rhythm.

This type of hunting was a delicate art. To the uninitiated observer, these moves looked simple; just a couple of people grinding. Some would say it was little more than clothed, public, vertical sex. Now granted, that was usually the initial goal, but Paul knew that in order for a guy to get what he wanted from a girl on the floor and eventually the bed, he had to be far more sensitive than that. He needed to read the girl's emotions and see what she wanted. It was important to at first impress, even disarm, with subtle but bold confidence. He then had to enter her rhythm and win her trust. In many ways hunting women was just like hunting any other animal. The predator had to carefully approach his target, for any unexpected movement could alert the prey to impending danger. But as long as the man could get close enough to strike, things fell into place. If he could do that, he could take a woman's heart. Well, at least for a night. And why would any guy want it for longer than that?

But this girl was different. He did not feel like he could dominate her rhythm. There was something else happening, but she was not distant either. Some girls would go to the clubs with more interest in dancing for its own sake than dancing with guys. They were the most frustrating. All they wanted was to be in rhythm with the music, and any guy entering the scene meant the girls had to be on guard. Now, of course, Paul thought he could break them down. Given the right circumstances he could seduce even prudish girls. The thing was, these kinds of girls just took longer. You had to spend the entire night focusing on just one. In the amount of time it took to get one girl's number who just wanted to dance, you could hook up with two or three loud, drunk sorority girls. Or, as Paul liked to think of it, these women were inferior investments.

But this woman was nothing like that. Although she was dancing in tune with the music, there was something more to her. Every time he tried to move close and control the rhythm, she countered, not by pushing him away like a prude, but by diving further still into the sound. Just as Paul tried to close in and start grinding, she would take a great leap and glide across the floor while spinning around. Next thing he knew, the girl was behind him and Paul would have to reset the rhythm and try again. At first, he thought she just had a couple clever moves which she could use to spin out of a grind, but the more he tried to lock her into place, the more she used grace and poise to escape his clutches.

She would turn around and make Paul think her guard was down as she glanced over her shoulder and summoned him with an alluring smile. Paul would move in for the kill, but it never worked. Just as he was about to start the seduction, she would twirl about and stand mere inches, sometimes less, away from him. The closeness of her movements would make Paul want to kiss her, but as he leaned forward she led him on until he had stepped into a new dance move. Suddenly, he found himself no closer to locking their bodies together, but still in tune with the music.

She was not dancing for the sake of hooking up with him; but she was not dancing for her own amusement either. It felt like she was trying to teach Paul how far dancing could go. Song after song he tried to change this woman from beautiful to sexy, but he never could lock her body into his own. Yet, all the while she kept drawing him further in. Several times as she arched around him, Paul could feel her skin brush past. He felt an increasingly powerful bolt of energy each time. It seemed like she was running through him like a breeze with even the most minor touch.

Finally, Paul decided to change his strategy. Apparently he could not attack this prey directly, for she was far too elusive. Instead, he decided to play her game. He would glide with her, lead her across the floor in great arching bounds, tip her back, and spin her around. The amazing thing was that the more he did this the more he forgot about the original goal. He stopped thinking about running his hands up and down the slender figure next to him and instead focused on leading her through increasingly complex motions. The more they danced the more he realized he could trust her kinetic energy. She was able to do whatever his hands asked her to. Backwards and forwards, up and down, everything he tried with her all felt right. Eventually, she jumped into his arms and he hoisted her into the air, spinning her around. He finally had her firmly within his grasp, but the thought of running his hands where they originally wanted to go never occurred to him. Instead, he only wanted to lift her higher into heaven. As Paul watched the maiden close her eyes and let her arms trail back like a swan gliding over a cool pond glistening in moonlight, he marveled at her beauty. There was something so majestic in the way she moved that he did not wish to disturb her motion.

The words in the songs flew by Paul. He never listened to lyrics while dancing. Active listening required steady minds, which usually meant still feet. He caught glimpses of phrases about power and praise, but nothing more. Finally, there was a break in the faster music and a slower song came on. The two pressed against each other as the neon lighting took on a softer hue. He wanted to talk to her, but for the first time in years a beautiful woman left him speechless. His stomach was in knots and his skin felt more sensitive than any dose of ecstasy. He held her close in their gentle slow dance. Eventually, she spoke up.

"You are a really good dancer." Paul was used to hearing that from girls, but this time he knew he did not deserve the compliment.

"No, you were really good. I was just trying to keep up. I have never seen anyone move like that before. It was like you were the music." She looked straight into his eyes and smiled. Although their tempo had slowed down, Paul's heart was speeding up. He was nervous, but his desire to talk outweighed his trepidation. "So, what was that secret you wanted to tell me?"

She rolled her eyes in a playful manor. "Oh, I think you'll have to guess."

Paul had absolutely no idea what she might be hiding, so he figured he would play things safe. "Were you by any chance going to tell me your name?"

She lifted her eyebrows as she flatly remarked, "What, you forgot?" Paul began to panic. The worst thing you could ever do while pursuing a girl was to forget her name. If you could not remember her name, how were you supposed to remember her birthday? Or ask her how her day went years down the road? Of course, Paul never had any intention of being there years down the road, or even the next morning for that matter, but the point was to make sure the girl never found that out. "You do remember that you were already given the answer earlier tonight. It was just a few hours ago. You said your name was Paul, and then you heard my name."

Paul thought he vaguely remembered getting her name, but right now his mind was drawing a blank. *Wow, I never thought I would regret getting so many girls in one night...*

She half giggled and said, "Well, I guess you'll just have to remember or wait."

Stupid, stupid, stupid! What is with me right now? I am totally off my game – getting out danced and forgetting the girl's name!

Sensing the thoughts running through Paul's head she said, "I guess you'll have to pay closer attention the next time someone tries to share with you. In the meantime, you'll have to work a lot harder to make up for lost ground."

Things had gone terribly wrong. He had let the perfect girl slip through his fingers and would have to spend more time tracking her down again. It was no matter; Paul was up for the task. He tried to play things cool. "So...how about that secret?"

She only shook her head. "No, no, no. Right now you do not even know the question. You'll have to figure out what you're asking before I can give you any conclusions." Hoping to finally get some answers out of this mystery, he confessed and laid his cards on the table.

"Alright, I know you want to play games, but I am really not tracking with you here. Maybe my brain's a little short wired or maybe you are just too beautiful for me to keep my mind working while you're around, but I'm really not sure what I am supposed to ask you." For several minutes the two had been dancing in tight proximity. Paul held her close while leaning against her. He was not sure what he had been feeling, but he knew he did not want these emotions to stop.

Paul never would have anticipated what she was about to say next. "Paul, the question...THE question, is Who Is GOD?" He stepped back and looked at her in befuddlement. "It's true, the question is: who is God?"

Now, not thinking about sex while dancing with a beautiful woman was fine. Bizarre, yes, but as long as you only did it occasionally and the girl was something really special you were still normal. Sometimes you just needed to let go of immediate physical gratification in order to achieve the bliss you were after. Chasing women was kind of like sports.

The batter does not self-consciously imagine himself swinging as he does so. Instead, he just follows what feels natural. Hitting one kind of home run with your body was similar to another. However, the last thing that Paul wanted to think about while dancing with a sexy lady was God. For crying out loud, you might as well bring the preacher into the room and let him chaperone!

"Wow, it looks like I just can't get away from this God stuff tonight. Look, I don't know if you are into that religion stuff or whatever, but I'm not. If you are than that's cool; it doesn't make much sense to me, but if it works for you than that's great. But I can't figure out why you would bring that up now! When I think about God, I think of crazy preachers with no life, not beautiful young women in fitting dresses out on a dance floor."

Once again the mysterious stranger drew close to him. "Well, then maybe you have misunderstood God. What do you imagine when you think of Him?" Paul tried to think of some polite way to put it, but there was no easy way to say this.

So with a much sterner voice than he planned, Paul spat, "When I think of God, I think of a stogy old man hanging out somewhere on a white puffy cloud who watches passively while humanity flounders in the dark. On a good day, we can forget about Him. On a bad day, we fight over some vague command that He probably never gave anyway and a bunch of people die. If He's up there, then He is little more than a grumpy guy who gets terribly offended when someone somewhere gives in to the nature He gave them and actually has a little fun." Paul suddenly became aware of how much louder his voice had grown. "Look, I like you, I really do. And sometimes belief in God really does help a person be a better person, but I just can't see the point."

A tear trailed down her cheek. As soon as Paul saw that tear his entire demeanor changed. He felt the tenseness in his shoulders that crept in during the God talk melt away. Suddenly, he was very sorry for what he said, or at least how he said it. He was not sure if he had done anything wrong per se, but he wished she would smile again so he asked, "Why are you crying?"

"I am crying because you cannot see what I am trying to show you. You look into the eyes of God and all you see are bloodshot orbs. I wish I could show you something more." Paul reached forward to wipe away the tear from her downcast eyes. In the process he ran his finger across her cheek and felt the sudden desire to kiss her again. This was different though. He did not want to kiss her just because she was beautiful, but rather because he wanted to make her feel whole again. Still, Paul thought better of it and held back. "Show me what you want me to see. I want to know what you believe."

She looked up and smiled. "Paul, God is a dancer."

Paul shook his head. "Now that I do not understand. Look at what you were doing a moment ago. Look at what we were doing. We were close, it was like we were one. When I first saw you I immediately knew how much I wanted to be near you. Through dancing we accomplished that. For an all too brief moment there was one person on the dance floor that just happened to have two bodies. But God would call that sinful. God would have us break all the dance floors into pieces and use the rubble to go build more hard church pews that children would be forced to sit quietly in while their mothers scolded them for misbehaving and their fathers fell asleep. God would silence the rhythm and divide us. God doesn't want to see us make something beautiful with our bodies, he just wants us to live in shame of the very thing that makes us beautiful. I can't picture any dancing in heaven, and I also can't picture any sex. God would cover our glory in shame, and I just don't see what's so great about a God who's such a prude that he can't bear to look at his own supposed image."

"Who told you God was like that? Was it God? Certainly not. God invented dancing. He made rhythm, and He made it in just such a way that we can access it. We can enter into rhythm because God wanted us to experience what the power of His patterns were like. God isn't ashamed of our rhythms. We might desecrate His artistry by smothering them in lust the way you did when you first saw me, but that is our shortcoming, not God's."

Paul blushed. Normally, the girl would never pick up on exactly what he was after until he had already taken it. But this one seemed to be on to him, she was inside his head and they both knew it.

"When you first began to dance with me all you could think about was sex. There was no love, just lust. You wanted to use something as perfect as rhythm to achieve an immediate, physical gratification at someone else's expense. I showed you how to lose yourself in the rhythm; how to vibrate into something larger than yourself. By the time we were done, it was not about the pleasure you were originally searching for; it was about something more. And ironically enough, that was more satisfying than the thing you first pursued." Paul took in his beautiful teacher's words like a gulp of ice cold water on a hot day. They felt so fresh they almost burned, but in a strange way he liked them. Dancing, just for the sake of being one with a larger rhythm and another...maybe he was just beginning to dance for the first time.

....

An old preacher sat beside the bed of a dying young man. He hardly knew the broken body in the bed before him. They had spent less than half an hour in dialogue, and even then Paul had been too bewildered to talk much. But at least a couple hours ago the young man was conscious. Now Paul lay with cracked ribs, head trauma, internal bleeding, and a number of other aliments which could not be easily medicated due to the drugs in his system. It was just over an hour from sunrise, and Mo was still uncertain that

Paul would ever see the light of day again.

Mo felt bad for the young man. What could have possibly gone wrong in his life to make him behave this way? How strange for a young person with his full years ahead of him to squander it like this. What would make someone spend night after night on those red light district street corners trading his life for a few cheap thrills? Now he clung to existence by a thread. Mo had spent the last couple hours reading to him from the book of Psalms. It was doubtful that Paul heard a word, but perhaps something would get through to him. Mo had finished reading the final psalm some time ago, but decided to read them again.

> Praise ye the LORD. Praise God in his sanctuary: praise him in the firmament of his power. Praise him for his mighty acts: praise him according to his excellent greatness. Praise him with the sound of the trumpet: praise him with the psaltery and harp. Praise him with the timbrel and dance: praise him with stringed instruments and organs. Praise him upon the loud cymbals: praise him upon the high sounding cymbals. Let everything that hath breath praise the LORD. Praise ye the LORD.

Mo closed his Bible and gathered his thoughts. "You

know Paul, there really is something quite beautiful about this whole music and dancing thing. People think that if it feels good than God wants you to stop, but that is nothing but the lie of the Devil. This psalm, like many of the others I read before it, takes joy in the creative expression of the body. I wish you were awake right now, because I think you would appreciate this point.

"You know, I had a wife some time ago. She has gone home to be with the Lord now, but she was an amazing dancer." Mo leaned back and folded his arms as he smiled in self-congratulation and chuckled. "You'd never know it by the little that's left of me, ah to be young and strong again... but back in the day I use to be pretty good too, if I do say so myself." Mo's smile faded as his eyes wandered off. "But she was amazing. I remember the first night we met, by the time we finished dancing I knew I was going to marry her." His gaze turned distant and he became silent before eventually returning to the hospital room with misty eyes. "So you see Paul, dancing is not wicked. It is nothing short of a gift from God."

Chapter 3 - God is a Musician

Paul sat in a large auditorium filled with thousands of people. In front of him stood all kinds of strange looking metallic scaffolding on top of a massive stage. Everyone around him seemed filled with anticipation. A familiar voice said, "Wow Paul, Mom would have loved to see this." Paul looked to his right and saw his father sitting with a stoic expression on his face. "I'm sorry," said his father as he cast his eyes down, "I shouldn't have brought that up." Paul thought the retraction was out of place and hardly worth apologizing for. After all, it had been several years...

No, it hadn't. His father was younger. The lines on his face were only beginning to form. This wasn't the ragged man that Paul had seen last Christmas, but the body that still carried some vitality in it; the body that had not yet grown old with the grief of his mother's death. Paul barely registered the sudden change in time and continued unabated. After recognizing his Dad's red "Jesus is the Reason for the

Season" sweatshirt, the motivation for his statement became obvious. Mom had always loved Christmas music. When she was alive their house was full of it all year round. They must be at a holiday concert.

There was little time to talk. A moment after Paul registered his father's comment the lights began to dim. The audience cheered as a man with long hair came up on stage with two men dressed like marines. The man explained he was from the Trans-Siberian Orchestra, and as was their custom, they were giving a small donation per ticket sold to a local charity; in this case Toys for Tots. The soldiers would be distributing the gifts to needy children all across the nation. It felt good to imagine all those poor children getting something for Christmas. The man quickly finished his speech, the marines left, and all became quiet.

And then it began. A wall of sound washed over them like a tidal wave. It hit them so hard that they could literally feel the music while scarlet red and blazing yellow lights twirled around bright blue. Great plumes of fire arose from the stage and cascaded into the air, smacking the audience with heat and making them marvel that the performers seemed unaffected. Men carrying electric guitars and women with the

voices of angels ran down the aisles. The metallic
scaffolding swung about carrying the performers
directly above the crowd. At one point snow, or at least
what looked like snow, fell from the sky. The
performance told several stories, all of which
contributed to the meaning of Christmas. By the time
it was over everyone was impressed, and Paul was
both exhausted and filled with adrenaline. He wanted
to stay, but it always seemed liked good things come to
an end.

On the way out Paul and his father discussed
the performance. Both agreed that it was superb, and
that they were very glad they came. When they
reached their car Paul's Dad did not turn the vehicle
on right away. Instead, he sat in silence gazing at the
night sky. Paul shifted in his chair as the
uncomfortable silence dragged on, and then the
interrogation began. "Hey Paul, can I ask you
something? Do you know who God is?" Paul rolled his
eyes. Just before Mom died Dad went on this major
God kick. On the one hand, Paul wanted to be
sensitive. After all, Mom meant the world to him. Most
of the best scores this old high school music teacher
had ever written were inspired by her, and deciding to

marry her was both the most impulsive decision he ever made (he purchased a ring after their first date), and the best.

Also, God was very important to Mom. She would wake early every morning just to pray for her husband and two boys. She wanted more than anything for the three of them to come to know God. Dad had patiently endured her piety for many years, but after her cancer set in he began to take it to heart. When Mom's body finally started to give in Dad was on his knees praying like a monk. It was understandable, the man was an artist. Those creative types often thought they had some special connection to the spiritual. Apparently, pretending reality had no rules helped one bend them. But now Mom had passed on and Dad had yet to come to his senses. He had begun to wake early and pray for his sons just like she had. Maybe walking in her footsteps made him feel like Mom was still close.

That was fine for Dad, but Paul just wanted to forget the whole thing. Mom was gone and she was no more coming back than the legions of other dead souls that had been prayed for over the eons. No matter how high people built their cathedrals the gargoyles still watched the graveyards fill. If ignoring that obvious fact helped you walk past the graveyard on your way to work than great, but the least you could do is keep your crutches to yourself. So Paul sat trapped. His Dad had the keys, it was dark out, and they had a long drive back home. He figured he would try to play things cool for a little while, but if Dad kept at this God stuff for too long he would push back. Prayer was meant to be silent and solo.

"No. I don't know who God is."

Paul's Dad leaned back and said nothing for a while. It almost looked like he was going to drop the subject, but apparently the old man could not resist the temptation. "I never used to buy into this whole God stuff myself. You know that. But the longer I live, the more I can't help but see the fingerprint of God everywhere I look, and hear His voice with every sound."

Paul had planned on waiting longer before going on the offensive, but his patience was already wearing thin. With a harsher voice than he intended Paul spat, "You know Dad, God isn't going to bring back Mom. You can wait, you can pray, you can stand on your head and pat your tummy while chanting Amazing

Grace for all I care, but SHE IS NEVER COMING BACK!" He felt years of frustration come pouring out and heard himself yelling. "She's DEAD! OKAY! Not a little dead, a lot dead. Dead dead. If you think you're going to see her again great. If you think that one day she is going to come home from work at the hospital just like she used to then I hope that keeps your dreams peaceful, but I don't need God to face reality!"

Paul's Dad seemed to barely register his son's resistance. Considering the boy's past behavior he probably expected as much. The old man continued. "Do you remember Mr. Weinberg? He was the physics teacher that came to your high school graduation. He teaches down the hall from me. Well, he told me something that I never knew before. Okay, I guess I might have studied it back in the day, but long story short I had forgotten about this stuff. Anyway, he said that the principles that underlie the frequencies in sound also match that of visible light. The science of it is really beyond me, but in a nutshell light and sound both work off a series of wavelengths and frequencies; the changes that alter music are the same kind of changes that alter color. Seeing and hearing are one in the same. They're two different ways of expressing patterns of information, of telling you something about the world.

"Mr. Weinberg also reminded me about atoms and molecules. Like I said, I haven't studied this stuff since I was in high school, but even I know that the way matter holds itself together is by vibrating. The electrons and protons and neutrons and so on in a given particle just keep on buzzing. The whole nature of creation is constantly vibrating at different frequencies. The light that we see and the matter that we touch is in the most literal sense a song. Kinda puts a new spin on things, doesn't it?"

Paul was confused and interested at the seemingly random tangent his father had just followed. This was unusually scientific for Dad. Paul knew he would regret it but couldn't help but ask, "So what's your point?"

Paul's Dad took a deep, slow breath before responding. It looked like he was carefully weighing his words. Who could blame him? Given Paul's past outbursts it was doubtful the boy was going to give his old man many chances to have calm conversations about God. "What we just heard...or saw, or both, was someone saying, or even singing, something. For that matter everything in reality is singing something. The whole world twirls around in a magnificent symphony and it all, as the Psalms tell us, 'declares the glory of God'."

Paul chuckled to himself. For a brief moment he almost sounded happy, but his laughter turned dark and cruel. "Wow, okay Dad." He responded with a sarcastic roll of his eyes. "I was wondering how you were going to connect that back to your question. Now let me throw some sound back at you. There's a song. She's a beautiful and, what did you say, a 'magnificent', song. She vibrates with a frequency that echoes about her until all her surrounding songs vibrate in harmony with her." Paul's voice became strained and intense. "And all the while there's this one conductor looking on, watching his song. He sees how beautiful she is, he sees her perfection. He sees how this song plays every note just as she should, how this song is the most beautiful of all. How even in the midst of this larger, greater symphony called reality there is no song which can match her beauty and grace. But what does the conductor do to his most prized and treasured song!? He lets her grow sick. He lets her decay. He lets her waste away in a hospital bed like a butchered slab of meat rotting under a hot desert sun. And all the while this conductor has the power to intervene at any given moment. He can stop this, but he chooses not to. He, for the sake of his own sick, twisted amusement, sits by and watches idly while his favored song is reduced to silence. And then all that's left when she's gone is an empty theater and a wretched conductor. If there is such a conductor then he's not worthy of worship, but I respect that beautiful song too much to say she suffered such a fate. So no, there is no such conductor...only the echoes of a now silent song."

Paul glared at his father like a trapped animal warning a predator to come no closer. He wanted nothing to do with these pretty analogies that did little more than package lies in fancy wrapping paper. Paul's Dad said nothing. Instead, he turned the car stereo on and let the words of music speak for him. The music he chose was very familiar. His mother used to play it often on their piano when she was still healthy enough to do so. It began as something dark and foreboding. Halloween had stolen its prologue for use in any number of hunted houses. But then the music changed. It became elegant and mysterious. It rose and sank like an intricate work of weaving. One could almost imagine the atoms all vibrating in unison with its grandeur playing in the background while the planets and galaxies did the same. The epic masterpiece came to a close and the silence it left only punctuated the power of what was heard.

"Johann Sebastian Bach wrote Toccata and Fugue in D minor to describe the glory of that infinite conductor. And that conductor lives, regardless of whether or not the audience would prefer silence. Your mother knew that, and one day, so will you." Only silence remained for the rest of the ride home.

....

Mo occupied a chair next to the hospital bed and night stand. On the night stand sat a radio just finishing a beautiful piece of classical music. He had been sitting by Paul for some time and had dozed off while listening to the radio. Now dawn was rapidly approaching, and he was glad to wake up when he did. "Oh yes. I love that piece. I'm no good at music, but if I could play a song, any song, only one song, that would be the one I would play. Well, I guess it's technically not a song since there are no words. Well, then again, I guess it is. Do you remember that Psalm I read some time ago, the one about the glory of God? Well, actually that probably doesn't narrow things down much. Here, let me find it." Mo grabbed his Bible and again flipped through the pages. "Ah, here it is!

> The heavens declare the glory of God; and the firmament sheweth his handywork. Day unto day uttereth speech, and night unto night sheweth knowledge. There is no speech nor language, where their voice is not heard. Their line is gone out through all the earth, and their words to the end of the world. In them hath he set a tabernacle for the sun, which is as a bridegroom coming out of his chamber, and rejoiceth as a strong man to run a race. His going forth is from the end of the heaven, and his circuit unto the ends of it: and there is nothing hid from the heat thereof. The law of the LORD is perfect, converting the soul: the testimony of the LORD is sure, making wise the simple. The statutes of the LORD are right, rejoicing the heart: the commandment of the LORD is pure, enlightening the eyes. The fear of the LORD is clean, enduring forever: the judgments of the LORD are true and righteous altogether. More to be desired are they than gold, yea, than much fine gold: sweeter also than honey and the honeycomb. Moreover by them is thy servant warned: and in keeping of them there is great reward. Who can understand his errors? Cleanse thou me

from secret faults. Keep back thy servant
also from presumptuous sins; let them not
have dominion over me: then shall I be
upright, and I shall be innocent from the
great transgression. Let the words of my
mouth, and the meditation of my heart, be
acceptable in thy sight, O LORD, my
strength, and my redeemer.

You know what I really love about Psalm 19? I mean,
they're all great, but in that Psalm you find this idea
that everything in creation, and I mean everything, is
always declaring the glory of God. Just image that.
Sunsets, words, stars...it all declares the glory of God.
Everything, and why? Because even the heavens
declare it, and no speech can be uttered that does not
sing it. There is nothing in all the world that does not
speak to us. Thunder might shout while a breeze
whispers, but ultimately it is all a word from God
above."

Mo shifted his weight. The monitors attached to
Paul had been stable for some time. It didn't look like
anything was changing. That was probably better than
nothing. The longer he lay there the more time his
body had to sew itself back together. Still, he feared for
the young man's mind. Could Paul hear anything the
preacher was saying? Or was he just a lifeless corpse,

little more than skin and bones but no mind, laying isolated from any sensations coming from the outside world?

Mo put his Bible aside and descended to his knees with clasped hands. His head nearly touched the cold tile floor as he bowed low. "Dear God, I do not know where this man's heart lay. From what I can gather it seems to be far from you, but I cannot tell. I also do not know if any words that I utter now reach him. Still, I ask that somehow, someway you do not abandon this child. Despite his foolish choices and his terrible predicament, I ask that you reach out to him. Show him that even in the darkness this world is still a painting, and that you are the painter. Pervade the inner recesses of his mind and memories and find him, in whatever dark place his consciousness now hides, for his salvation, and your glory, Amen."

Chapter 4 - God is a Painter

The campus was huge, but such should be expected
from a well-endowed research university. Building
after building filled with classrooms, dormitories, and
labs dotted the landscape. The campus formed a city
of science that represented just how far technology
had come. This particular building, however, focused
more on the cultural than the empirical. The multi-
level museum/department of creative arts was replete
with various kinds of expression. This specific hallway
showed paintings and sculptures from different
peoples and time periods. If one started at the far end
and worked his way up the hall, he could survey the
artistic development of humanity, from cave drawings
through Athens and just past the renaissance. Then, if
he turned around and walked back down the hall
along the other wall he could view the transitions from
modernism, to post modernism, and finally end with
the present.

At this point in the semester Paul really should

have been studying for finals, but several hours of trying to crack organic chemistry had left him more frustrated than educated. So he slowly meandered through this building, glancing at what geniuses of another stripe had created. Some of the images procured an immediate reaction. He had spent a lot of time staring into the portrait of George Washington crossing the Delaware with awe. The man looked fearless and powerful, and despite the fact that Paul had seen this painting numerous times in history books, he could not help but be impressed. Other works confused him, or at least left him with absolutely no reaction. No matter how long he looked at the Mona Lisa he couldn't see anything but a very plain woman staring back at him. Still, she was far more attractive than a plastic model of a carbon molecule.

The current images he was staring at formed an odd couple. To the left sat a black and white photograph of a rustic looking cottage. It looked like it would make a decent hunting lodge. There were probably moose heads mounted to the walls inside and bear skin rugs on the floors. Great trees surrounded the building, and given the backdrop, it was evidently located in the mountains. Outside a couple hunters were skinning a wolf carcass. They were half way through their grisly task, as was evident by the partially naked animal lying on the ground in a pool of blood. But the lack of color subtracted from the picture's gore. One immediately knew that the gray pool must have been blood, but without its distinctive scarlet red, the blood looked more like something spilling out of an ink well than an animal.

Next to this black and white image sat an incredible collection of color. A painting of a wooded cottage that was drenched in so much light it almost looked as if the house and surrounding floral shimmered like the sun. The spectrum was so exaggerated that it seemed as if a child had picked out the painter's colors. Yet somehow the nearly surreal image remained realistic, almost like there had been a continuum between the real world and the dream world, and that the artist had chosen to plant his painting on the boarder in-between the two. One more speck of color and it would have been too perfect, and one less and it would have been believable. The name on the plaque beneath the painting said, "Thomas Kinkade".

The two images contrasted sharply with one another. One attempted to show things as they are after being stripped of their color. The other exaggerated color to the point of incredulity. They formed a comparison of detached realism versus wishful bliss. Paul wasn't exactly sure what he was supposed to feel, but he knew that the way the two images coincided depressed him. They seemed to form a chasm between what was and what could be. Or perhaps the situation was more hopeless than that. Perhaps the chasm was between what was and what would never be?

"What do you think of those two?" Paul spun around. A middle-aged woman in the formal attire expected of the gallery's curators stared directly into the display.

"Well, I'm not quite sure what I'm looking at," responded Paul. "Most of the other images here hit you with a message from the artist. But this display is playing tricks on me. Neither the photographer nor the painter ever wanted their work to be placed alongside the other one. I feel like there's a new meaning that develops; a second layer of purpose that was never there to begin with. Maybe the photograph was supposed to show how we struggle for survival with the rest of the animals. And maybe the painting was there to tell us that man is at his best when he lives in harmony with the wild. But when you put the two of them next to each other, the original meaning is lost. Something else emerges."

The woman stroked her chin and nodded. She seemed to approve of the assessment while judging it through a very experienced and learned grid. "So what is the emergent meaning?" she asked. Paul hesitated before answering. He was confident he knew what the painting meant to him, but was not sure if this same meaning would be anything but rudimentary to an experienced art critic. Then again, in art could anyone be wrong?

"I see the meaning as something dark. To the left there's real life, to the right, a dream. The two don't intermingle, and there's no way to bridge the gap. It kinda reminds me of when a DJ mixes several songs that were never supposed to blend together. You can completely change the feelings associated with a particular set of words just by reworking the background sounds. An upbeat song can become slow and sad, or a sad song can become sensual, or whatever. But you will lose the original meaning if the new sound does not fit the old lyrics. Now look at this happy go lucky painting. It starts to seem dreary when contrasted with the grays and blacks of the photograph. In a weird sort of way the colors look even less colorful then the black and white would have appeared in isolation."

The lady frowned. "My, my, that is a depressing thought. Why don't you think of things in a little more positive way? How about this? To the left we see an admittedly cold, gritty reality. This reality lives in the shadow of something beautiful, but by itself could never aspire to such beauty. Luckily, it need not live in isolation of its dreams and aspirations. The difficult particulars that struggle in black and white need not be separated from the beautiful universals that flood the ideal. Does that sound like an equally plausible interpretation to you?"

Paul shrugged. "Yeah, I guess so."

The woman laughed. "But I suppose this is finals time, so all looks dark and dreary; even a Thomas Kinkade painting." Paul shrugged again.

"So why does this Kinkade guy paint that way?" The woman took a step closer to the painting. She was only a couple feet away and meticulously judging every detail.

"Well, this painter is unlike the majority of other contemporary artists you will see in the gallery. Most art in the postmodern era communicates a very negative and downcast message. There is an undeniable futility in calling a signed urinal or a crucifix dunked in that nasty stuff art. Some would even call it anti-art. But Kinkade is different. He strives to show people that behind life there is a certain beauty and grandeur. He depicts reality at its best, its most idealistic, in order to show people the beauty of God's work."

Paul contorted his face and folded his arms. "Well, no wonder why I don't like it then. All warm fuzzies and no real life." The art critic stepped back and stared at Paul. She eyed him up, apparently trying to ascertain the cause of his drab disposition. "I tend to think that your negative assessment of this positive art transcends the draining sphere of pressure from finals."

Paul laughed and shook his head. "Yeah, you got that right. Look, maybe I sound like a bit of a downer, but I don't see the point behind this kind of fantasy.

Reality is a cold, dark, harsh place. Things don't turn out the way you want, people don't stick around, and at the end of all the struggle and pain we wind up like that wolf carcass over there. No matter how much we try to deny it, we're just animals. That's all we are. We want to fight, feed, and the other f-word. Beyond that is nothing but a bunch of fairytales."

The woman stared directly into Paul's eyes. He noticed that she had two different colored pupils, one slate gray and the other bright blue. "You know they call this painter the 'Painter of Lights'. His work is meant to emanate the light of Christ and shine into the dark places in our lives."

Paul laughed out loud with a smile that began genuine but quickly turned sadistic. "Jesus huh? No wonder the joy seems so fake. It's hard to find happiness in a dead guy on a cross."

The curator responded both sternly and in a matter of fact tone. "No, that is not true. It is impossible to find long lasting joy in death isolated from resurrection."

Paul wasn't prepared for the force of the rebuttal. Something about this woman seemed stronger than he'd expected. Usually when he thought

of an older woman talking about the beauty of God, he
imagined a grandmother baking cookies or something
equally disgusting in a cute kind of way. They would
usually drag your ear through the mud with overly
sentimental emotional appeal rarely, if ever,
punctuated by a good argument. He had not
anticipated breaking into a debate over the meaning of
death with an educated stranger. Still, he decided that
correcting stupidity was more noble than tolerating it
long enough for folly to propagate.

"Hard to find joy isolated from resurrection, eh?
Well maybe I'm just mistaken, but I sure think the
world would be a happier place if no one had ever tried
to burn any witches, kill any Indians, run any
crusades, or throw anyone on the rack in an
inquisition." Paul tried to start out cautious. He had
no idea who this woman was or what information she
might have to work with, so he wanted to advance a
level headed, sober position. Still, somewhere in the
back of his mind Paul knew his disdain for God was
bleeding through.

"You're an art curator. I assume that means
you've spent a lot of time around universities, probably
have a Ph. D., and have read tens of thousands of

pages on art history. You're an accomplished, successful woman. And I think that's great. But there was a time when people, especially people in the church, would not have thought so, and they were pretty aggressive when sharing their resentment. Back in the day when they wanted to punish a woman for being independent and free from the church's bonds, they would take a lovely torture device that looked like a pear made out of different plates at the end of a shaft. They would insert this object in some place better left unnamed amongst polite company and begin unscrewing it. The plates of the pear would begin to separate. It would literally break the pelvis from the inside out. Real nice, don't cha think? Done so that hags, oh and that used to be a positive term similar to sage until the church's propaganda machine perverted it... so that hags and witches and such were kept in line. And do you know what the best part of the whole damn thing was? I think an artist like yourself will appreciate this; the image of Jesus was placed on those metal plates, just to make sure you didn't forget that it was Jesus who was literally screwing you over in more ways than one. That's not happiness, and it's not life either."

Who is God?

The curator nodded her head and grunted. She had neither winced nor blinked during Paul's diatribe. Instead, she found his argument to be lacking in historical analysis and heavy on emotional appeal, but nevertheless rational enough to at least warrant response. She walked past Paul without making eye contact while pausing for a moment to utter, "Come." She continued to walk until she reached the hall's end. Paul was tempted to run in the opposite direction. He didn't know what she had to show him, but was confident that whatever it was, it was probably not worth seeing. Curiosity, however, got the better of him and he followed. *Why do I get the feeling that I'm being led like a sheep to the slaughter*, thought Paul as his footsteps echoed in the hall. The curator continued with a military like steadiness. Paul thought she was going to walk directly into the hall's far wall until she abruptly turned on her heel. And then the lesson began as the two started moving down the hall and the steady speech of the curator filled the room.

"To the left we see the earliest form of art of which we have record; namely cave drawings. The figures are gaunt and anything but lifelike. They are little better than charcoal stick figures. The images depicted are typically mundane – mostly hunting and fishing. There is little in this art that shows evidence of abstract reasoning. If humanity did engage in such activity at this point in history, the primitive state of art did not allow such thoughts to be communicated via the medium of painting. As you can see, what little sculpture existed did no better with its bones and beads.

"But as time passed society advanced. Hunters and their tribes grew into civilizations, and then began working with metals like copper. This opened new doors for artistic expression. Also, art took on grandiose measures in the form of architecture. First, things like Stonehedge came. Then step pyramids, temples, and· eventually even the great pyramids at Giza. Large empires such as the Sumerians, Egyptians, Assyrians, Babylonians, and Phoenicians developed. These peoples created powerful nations that dominated their surroundings. During the apex of their respective dynasties no one dared oppose them.

"However, their power and influence would all eventually be surpassed by the two most unlikely of peoples. The more western of these were the Greeks. With their emphasis on philosophy, a love of knowledge spread across their culture. Great centers of learning developed and shared the teachings of men like Plato and Aristotle. Whereas the Egyptian statues were block like and too irregular to look real, the artistic expressions born in Greece produced statues that actually looked like real people. For the first time art really began to model nature. Despite the small size of Greece, its cultural impact would surpass any of its larger neighbors.

"All the while another group began to take form. This kingdom was the most diminutive and insignificant. Even Greece possessed a more formidable fighting force. They consisted of a dozen small tribes that spent most of their time either squabbling among themselves or surrendering to their neighbors. And yet, of all the ancient peoples it is only Israel that survived. Israel usually did not invest its resources into grand buildings or powerful armies. Although their temple was extraordinary, and they did occasionally win a war, Israel, more than any of its rivals, put its faith in God's word. Their people trusted that no matter what happened God would eventually deliver them.

"Israel looked at the world in a radically different

way from her peers. Her neighbors saw their king as
the image of the lead god. Just as a divine hierarchy
existed in the heavens, man was to build a new
hierarchy on earth. By this divine right, the priest king
did as he saw fit, and to disobey him was to disobey
the gods. But Israel divided its power into the three
sacred offices of prophet, priest, and king. No one man
was allowed to fill all three roles. The divine did not
only dwell in the king; instead, all of humanity was the
image of the one true high God. This idea, despite
centuries of slavery and failure, united the Israelites
with the belief that even those at the base of the pagan
pyramid still mattered in the eyes of God. Israel paid
the price for its revolutionary theology. It incurred the
vitriolic hatred of its enemies when it refused to
submit.

"But God did not abandon Israel. Even with
their precarious position between the Assyrians above
and the Egyptians below, this miniscule people has
survived to this day. The Romans were the children of
the Greeks, and they brought Greek thought across
the map as they modeled their empire under the
intellectual guidance provided by their philosophical
forefathers. However, the Jews trusted not in their

isolated cognitive capacities but in piety. The thinkers of the Old Testament are found in the author of Job and the wise king Solomon. Their artistic expression lay in their scriptures which were carefully guarded. Every letter was counted, every line of poetry measured, so much so that a scribe would rather destroy years' worth of work than let a single false stroke of the pen survive and potentially be incorporated into the cannon by mistake.

"Just as the speculative ideas of the Greeks subsumed and outlasted the armies and economies of the empires, the conviction of the Jews would subsume and outlast the Greeks. Eventually the classical world collapsed from its own greed, and in its wake stood a series of teachings which were guarded over by the church. As the Greco Roman pillars fell into disuse the flying buttresses of the great cathedrals took their place. The architectural marvels of the bygone era were combined with new developments in painting. Whereas the predecessors never advanced past flat, two dimensional painting indicative of the Egyptian statues, the Christian era saw the rise of the Sistine Chapel. Likewise, while the Romans never saw fit to see a slave as equal to a free man, slowly the dominated slave evolved into the right bearing serf. Forerunners of later progress were found in the magna carter and other great works, but alas, we move too quickly."

In the time needed for the two to reach the end of the hallway they had already covered human history up to the middle ages. They had passed by ancient masks, burial garments, amulets, paintings, and model temples. Now they transitioned from one wall to its parallel companion and began retracing their steps while observing the objects lining the other side. All Paul had gathered thus far was that a series of ancient empires attempted to control others with raw power and had eventually been forgotten. However, a couple smaller groups dominated ideas and we are still talking about them. But what did any of that have to do with the Thomas Kinkade painting or God?

"The same idea which eventually destroyed the divine right of kings, which the Christians had inherited from the pagan belief that the Roman emperor was a god, would soon turn the world upside down. By again embracing the Old Testament notion that man was made in the image of God, he simultaneously provided the intellectual foundation for saying that every man, even the peasant, is valuable, and that every man, even the king, will be judged by God. The great Puritan philosopher Samuel Rutherford turned the authority of the king against himself with his monumental text, *Lex Rex*, in which he argued that just as the Old Testament king was no greater than the prophet and priest, and like them under God's authority, so was the modern king. The idea shattered the prevailing political systems and produced both the constitutional republic and the art which we now see."

The curator stopped and gestured toward the patch of wall next to them. The art of the renaissance, reformation, and enlightenment told a story. At first, there was a dramatic increase in the sophistication of the painting. Each successive work seemed to build on what came before and produced something more lifelike. But then the theme of the art changed. The earlier depictions were mostly grandiose religious images. Jesus, the lamb, or something to that affect, took center stage while angels would fly overhead and the people in the foreground looked on. However, somewhere between guys like Rembrandt and Picasso the paintings shifted towards increasingly mundane topics detached from reality.

Paul began walking forward. He was no longer following his impromptu instructor, but instead cutting across the wide swaths of history on his own. The art was changing. People no longer looked so noble. They became increasingly abstract as crystal-clear images turned to vague impressions, which were then followed by even more abstract cubes and lines. A supposedly nude woman coming down the stairs was really just a collection of shapes. Another allegedly scientific painting replaced every single brushstroke with a dot in order to mimic pixels in the eye. It cast away the great detail of the past in its effort to replace tradition with scientific precision. Eventually, the paintings were just splashes of color thrown against a canvas, or even just a single, blue canvas. And sure enough both the urinal with a signature and the crucifix drowned in a bottle of the artist's urine were also there. Near the end of the hall sat a small set of dirty, intertwining plumbing pipes mounted to a wooden box. The piece was dated from 1917 and titled, "God." Finally, Paul came back to where he had started and stared again at the Kinkade next to the black and white photograph.

A door just a couple feet away from Paul swung

open and a young man walked by. His hair was died electric blue and formed a spiked mohawk. He wore a t-shirt saying, "Against All Authority" under his leather jacket, which was covered in metal studs and patches with various band labels. Tattoos and piercings ran up and down his body. The young man walked by without saying a word and reached for a pack of cigarettes as he passed. Paul watched him move down the hall and leave on the far end. He might as well have stepped out of one of the postmodern paintings.

"You see Paul, what Kinkade was doing with those pretty lights was something very radical. He was returning to a time when people looked out at nature and saw beauty and wanted to express that beauty in their own creative acts. The so-called art of our own era rebels against this. It instead sees only absurdity and chooses to express that absurdity. There is no God, and there are no absolutes. Man is free to create whatever image he wants, no matter how shocking, for who could ever tell him to do otherwise. Ironically, in an age of drugs, sex, and rock and roll, the most unique and individualistic thing an artist, or for that matter anyone, can do is follow the rules. What Kinkade does by trying to express something that fills the viewer with God's peace is a subtle way, or I guess when transposed against the rabble of his era a not so subtle way, of choosing to follow his Creator in an ordered action that harmonizes with the cosmos instead of jarring with them in an act of chaos."

Paul's head was spinning. The Kinkade painting did possess a certain innocent joy that the other modern images around it lacked. But what did that show? That God was a painter? That painters who followed him did the best painting? That seemed like a tenuous connection, but looking back over the history of artistic expression lent credit to this lofty claim. Paul began to think back to discussions he remembered with his Dad. The old man was convinced he had seen something similar in music. According to his father, music had climbed to an artistic majesty during the Christian era which it left during the recent time of rebellion. He had said at several points that all one needed to do was compare Bach and the club music that Paul liked dancing too in order to "feel" the difference between divinely inspired art and secular insanity. The argument had always struck Paul as ad hoc, but the more he thought about it now the more it started to make sense.

Paul placed his hand against the wall next to the Kinkade painting and stared deeply into its rich pigment. *I wonder if this is what runs through my Dad's mind when he composes music. Does he feel like a little child of God busily emulating his Father's work? But the more fun you make it the more pagan it becomes. If we are so divine why do we need to copy what some distant architect did? Why should we even care? Why can't we just do our own thing and express our individuality as we choose? If God really wanted creatures to do as he did, why didn't he make a bunch of photocopiers?*

But as Paul's mind began a counter argument the pigment before him started to change. The image blurred and the colors ran together. Contrasts faded as everything took on the ashen-gray of the photograph and Paul's thoughts began to waver. The strange place where he stood that lay somewhere between a dream and the horizon began to break down.

. . . .

The heart monitor next to Paul began beeping erratically. Mo bolted to the control panel next to Paul's bed and pushed the call button for a nurse. He then left the room and hurried down the hall. Paul was crashing, and Mo was not sure if he would ever wake up.

Chapter 5 - God is Light

Ocean waves massaged the shoreline as the breeze carried the smell of fresh, salty air to Paul's nostrils. There was a peace and tranquility that wiped away the odd sense of a growing distance from somewhere. Across the ocean, the faint glow which heralds the arrival of the sun was just beginning to form. Paul smiled as the coming warmth filled his soul while the light filled the sky. He ran his bare feet through the sand and felt the tiny cool grains in between his toes. Invigoration heightened his senses while contented peace calmed his mind.

A familiar voice spoke. "Hey handsome, care if I join you?"

Paul turned and saw the woman from the club. She was dressed differently, but looked just as stunning. She wore the same ornate necklace with three triangular prisms bound by silver around her neck. Her blue outfit was replaced by a bright yellow summer dress covered in flowers. She wore a wide brimmed, light brown hat made of a woven, natural ribbon. The warm colors cascading across the sky mixed well with her healthy complexion. Paul smiled as his eyes took in the full sight of her. The first time he saw her he believed he was looking at a goddess fit for a temple. Now he saw an angel fit for heaven.

"It would be an honor to be comforted by your presence", he charmed.

And with that, the young woman sat on the sand about a forearm away from Paul, facing the ocean and the rising sun. Paul was not sure what to do next. He was elated to be in her presence once more, but nervous and unsure of what to say. He thought of complimenting her eyes, and mentioning how they contrasted nicely with her attire, but thought that might seem like a pick-up line. He considered complimenting her hat, but figured that sounded like something only a guy with a "fabulous" fashion sense would say, and he did not want to give her the wrong impression. The suave sayings that normally rolled off his tongue seemed to shrivel until all that was left was a giddy, unsteady, school boy. Finally, he said the one thing that he would immediately regret asking.

"So are you still mad at me for forgetting your name?" *No! Stupid, stupid, STUPID! Why would you say that!*

She gave him a sly smile. "Well, I guess that depends on whether you remember it now." Paul panicked as his mind desperately searched for something to help him remember. When did he first meet her? At what point would he have asked? His memory still seemed foggy, and he could not afford to fail after he just voluntarily put his head on the chopping block, but the seconds wore on too long.

"I guess that means no." The lady sighed as she rolled her eyes. "Well that's a pity. If you could remember my name then maybe I would give you my number, that way we could talk. But how are we supposed to make good conversation if you cannot even remember a little thing like that." She sighed again... "Oh well." The young woman shifted her weight and stood up to leave. Paul moved to his knee and prepared to follow.

"Please don't go! I know I'm not very good with names. I know I should remember. Please, trust me, I wish more than anything right now that I could. But I can make good conversation. What would you like to talk about?"

Under other circumstances, this player would be disgusted with himself. Here he was, begging for a woman to stay. This behavior totally violated the most basic laws of male-female interaction. It was a rarely known fact that the attractiveness of a man is inversely proportional to how nice and predictable the guy is. A man who would buy a girl flowers on her birthday, never cheat, and always ask how a woman's day went was boring. At most he would be put in the gay best friend category and have to endure the girl's tears as she cried over the most recent bad boy stud who had stolen her heart. Hence, it paid to be the bad boy. But here was Paul, head honcho and top gun, forgetting all that he had ever learned about the delicate art of manipulating beautiful women.

"Well...why don't you talk about the sunrise?" She suggested as she sat back down. Paul glanced over at the rising sun. *Good, this is good. We can work with this.* He slowly sat back down next to her.

"The sunrise? Yeah, the sunrise. Impressive how it works in connection with the ocean below it. In isolation the two are both beautiful. The ocean represents a vast expanse of something deep and teaming with mystery; you have to plunge its depths to discover its treasures, while the sun possesses its own grandeur. One must instead receive the outward energies of the sun in order to enter its depths. When the two are put together, they form a wonderful couple, a new, delicate pair that dance as the sparkling waters reflect back the rays of her warm companion."

"My, my Paul, how romantic."

Paul smiled as he wrapped his arms around his knees.

"But I'm still mad at you for forgetting my name." She teased with a friendly punch to his arm. Paul frowned.

"Oh don't look so upset Paul, I was only kidding ...mostly." She smiled mischievously. The tip of the sun was climbing over the horizon and lighting up the sky with ever greater glory. Suddenly an idea popped into Paul's mind.

"I have a question. Do my eyes reflect the sunrise?" For a moment their eyes met before she glanced away and teasingly swatted his hand.

"Oh that's so cliché. You just wanted me to look into your eyes!"

Paul smiled again. "Well, actually, I was hoping you would let me look into yours. And you did, so cliché or not, it still worked." They both smiled and stared deeply into each other's eyes, this time watching the sunrise from a new perspective.

Paul could feel his heart flutter the same way it had when they danced. He felt knots growing in his stomach as he caught her floral fragrance in the air. Paul didn't realize how close he was moving towards her until his forehead bumped against the rim of her hat. Breaking the tension, she pulled back and laughed at Paul's awkward motion. His shoulders slumped as she smiled at him.

"Ya know, this is all your fault." He said sheepishly.

"My fault! She placed her left hand over her heart with an air of innocence. "How is any of this my fault? What are you blaming me for?" Paul ran his fingers through his hair as he collected his thoughts. In this situation, Paul would normally try to shift the blame to the girl. That would put her on the defensive and be ever so slightly mean. This would allow him to utilize the inverse relationship between niceness and desirability that all women see in men. If he kept going on about beauty and sunsets, he would be doomed to the friends category. Or, at the very least have to court this girl for weeks, maybe even months, before getting what he wanted.

The funny thing was, he didn't mind that idea. The notion of just talking to this mysterious stranger for hours struck Paul as an enjoyable pastime in itself. He was tempted to do the one thing that no player under any circumstances is ever to do, upon pain of castrating one's masculinity and forever sentencing himself to the drab world of emo music and, hell forbid, poetry. Paul decided to tell her the truth.

He smiled, returning the friendly punch he received before. "I'm blaming you for making me act so awkward. If you were any other girl, I wouldn't feel so nervous. I mean, here we are on a beach with a beautiful sunrise. Any normal guy sitting next to a girl as gorgeous as you would be asking himself how to make his next move, but I feel so nervous that I can't even stop myself from head-butting your hat." A crisp breeze fluttered across the beach before she responded.

"That was cute. Maybe I will tell you my name after all. But first I need to know whether or not you have found an answer to the question." Paul rolled his eyes as his stomach sank. "Let me guess, the question about 'Who is God?' right?"

She folded her arms, "Don't sound too excited." Paul knew he should have responded more gracefully, but this recurring God business kept driving him mad.

"Look, you told me that God was like a dancer. And ya know, let's say for the sake of argument that he is. In fact, let's say that he's like music and a painter – he's a great artist and all the world is his stage. That all sounds great, but can't you people ever just enjoy something beautiful in and of itself? I mean, look at this beach and that amazing sunrise. Isn't that wonderful? Why do we need to bring God into this?"

The woman reached to her necklace and unlatched it. She held it out in front of her and let the light shine through it. The power of the light made the object sparkle like something out of a dream. The necklace seemed to dance in the sunlight the way the waves did. She turned the necklace to and fro, each time sending a new collection of colors running up and down its length. Paul knew when he saw the jewelry that it would glisten in the sunlight. What he did not expect was for the glass to refract the light like a prism and cast the already impressive morning light into an array of colors that fluttered about the beach behind them. The anger stirring in Paul's heart from thoughts of God quickly subsided as amazement replaced the swollen void.

"Paul, do you know how light works?" The young man shook his head, partially out of honesty but mostly out of a desire to hear this woman's voice. "Light exists in a spectrum. There are many shades which are spread out over a spectrum of wavelengths. The energy comes to our eyes in different frequencies, which we see as different colors. Red is red and yellow is yellow because red vibrates one way and yellow vibrates another way. Those prisms take white light, which is a composite of all the colors, and separates it into distinctive shades. White light has a little blue in it, some green, purple, and a little bit of every color across the spectrum. That's why the three primary colors of blue, yellow, and red can make any of the others. So, in one color there can be others, and when colors mix, new unexpected colors emerge. White light weaves them all together, and prisms break them down into their components."

Paul looked up from the newly grafted rainbows

and into her eyes again. "That was beautiful," he said entranced by her words. "So beautiful that I think there's only one place fit for this necklace to rest." Paul took the collection of prisms from her hands and moved towards her. He carefully placed the necklace around her neck, reaching behind her to reconnect its latch. He leaned over her shoulder in order to see where the two sides of the chain should meet. She did not pull away, but instead allowed Paul to come closer. After reconnecting the latch Paul pulled his head back, but kept his hands wrapped around her neck. He paused and waited to see her reaction. Would she grow tense and uncomfortable? Pull away? Push him off?

No, she let their eyes meet and smiled. Paul's restraint melted before his mounting passion. His body leaned forward and he closed his eyes. She let the tension build, but was not sure yet if he was ready to kiss her. Rather than pulling back though, she challenged him just as his lips were mere inches from hers.

"God is light."

Paul's eyes shot opened. "What?"...

"That's the answer to the question. God is light."

Paul pulled away and lay down in the sand. He

groaned, "Okay, so God is like light. Light is pretty and so is God, right? Is that the connection? Please tell me it is so that I can tell you I get it and we can move onto another conversation topic." Now it was her turn to lean in as she rested her arms against Paul's chest.

"Well, you have the right frequency but the wrong instrument...at least we're making progress."

Paul rolled his eyes again. "You do realize that if it were not for your insane beauty...well that and your intoxicating scent...okay and your amazing dancing... Look, if you weren't you, I would roll over and walk away right now."

She mockingly pouted and asked, "Oh why is Paul so grumpy?"

In a strained voice Paul fired back, "I just don't understand this whole God thing. You say that God is like light. Well, maybe, but then why does God want to keep us in the dark? Why is it that this being of light doesn't tell us why we suffer, or what we are supposed to do, or any of the other things which you would think an enlightened being might want to share with his children. For crying out loud there's a reason why they call the Christian era the 'Dark Ages' and its end the 'Enlightenment'."

She smiled back at him and said nothing for a long time. "You know you're really kind of cute when you're angry," she stated, breaking the building silence with a return to playful banter. "I would prefer it if you smiled more but you're still cute." Paul half laughed at her attempt to lighten the mood.

"Paul, I think you're approaching this all wrong. You've heard of the Trinity, right?" Paul reluctantly nodded. "Okay, so God is triune. There are three persons in Him. There is a Father, and a Son, and the Ghost. All three are fully God, but all three are distinct."

Paul raised his brow as he interjected. "Alright, let me guess where this is going then. God is like light in that there are three persons in God, whatever that means, just like there are three primary colors."

The young woman shook her head. "Yes but no. Or maybe I should say yes, but that is not enough. You see, light is the result of a relationship. Yes, there are distinctions within it. There are shades of color, or frequencies, with their own respective areas of focus. But that's not all that there is. The final product is greater than the sum of its parts. The final product is a relationship, it's something that comes from the unity of those respective diversities in a way that is analogous to two dancers that vibrate into one perfect harmony."

Paul let those words slide across his mind and settle in. "So are you telling me that when you say God is like dancing, and when you say that God is like light, what you are ultimately getting at is that God is a relationship?" Her eyes lit up brighter than the rising sun behind her as she grabbed his shirt.

"Yes, YES! That's exactly it! God, in His nature, in His essence, is an inherently relational being. He is a being that exists in harmony with Himself. We would also be in harmony with Him if we would only let ourselves fall into proper rhythm with Him."

Paul leaned over on his side. Both lay next to each other in the sand. "You really like these analogies, don't you?"

Her excitement continued as she struggled to contain herself. "Of course! I mean, think about it. All of creation reflects the Creator. It's through light, which is perhaps more like God than any other part of it, that we are enlightened and see what God would have us see. It's through this light, or rather through this relationship in another form, that we can see how

God relates to ourselves. Don't you think that's beautiful?"

Paul paused. She seemed on the verge of ecstasy and he did not want to disappoint her. He raised his hand and brushed his fingers down the length of her cheek before twirling his finger around her hair. "So you're telling me that all this is about a relationship."

"Yes, that's right," she whispered.

He slowly shifted his weight and leaned in closer to her. She lay on her back while Paul leaned over her, resting his weight on one arm while the other continued to play with her hair. She reached up and placed her hand on his side. Thoughts began racing across Paul's mind. *She must want me to kiss her. She keeps flirting with me and letting me touch her. Now she has finally put her hand on me, and I am close enough to....*

Just before their lips met Paul halted. For a moment they sat suspended in anticipation as their breathing grew heavy. He wanted to kiss her. He wanted to enter into relation with this woman. He wanted to begin slowly at first, and then kiss her more deeply until the two performed a second dance. This one would be under light, just as the first had been within music. The dance would be just as enthralling and even as spiritual as the first.

But Paul hesitated. He knew what he wanted, but there was something else he needed first. He softly whispered, "You know it's kinda hard to enter into a relationship with someone who you can't even call by name." Paul began to feel confident. It had seemed like he had lost his bearings with this girl and was completely out of control, but now he thought that he just might be able to start solving this mystery.

She rubbed her face against Paul's hand and let his palm slowly cup itself around her cheek. She closed her eyes and lost herself in the thrill of his touch. He knew how much he wanted to hear her answer and desperately wished she would end his waiting. But he also knew that she, like him, had chosen to let the ecstasy of the moment build. Paul could feel his restraint melting as her perfection filled him with desire. He knew if she did not speak soon his discipline would buckle and their lips would meet before he found his answer. His lips grazed hers like a feather barely breaking the film over still water, but still he never truly kissed her. With a voice short of breath and equally invigorated by growing desire the young woman whispered back, "Paul...my name is Grace."

....

Moses had been busily praying for the nearly dead man in front of him. Why was God doing this? If God would only awaken the poor soul for but a brief time Moses could share the gospel with him. Instead, the old preacher sat talking to what looked like a mindless body. At this point, it was hard to tell whether Mo was preaching to save a soul or to prevent boredom as the hours passed by in near silence. He had several times considered giving up and leaving. At least at home he could sleep in a real bed instead of a chair commandeered from the lobby, and with Paul probably brain dead what difference did it make anyway?

The last episode had been disastrous. He was not sure what drugs the doctors had pumped into Paul, but he knew they must have been pretty desperate to put so much more poison in his already taxed system. One of the nurses seemed hesitant to obey the doctor's orders as they rolled him into the emergency room, but the drop in Paul's heart rate had apparently left them no choice. Now, several hours later and after extensive prayer Paul was even closer to death. Still, the preacher persisted.

> Then spake Jesus again unto them,
> saying, I am the light of the world: he that
> followeth me shall not walk in darkness,
> but shall have the light of life.

"You see Paul...wow, I really hope you can hear what I'm saying right now. Anyway, you see Paul, Jesus Christ is the light of the world. It is He that makes sense out of all that we are and all that we do. If Jesus had never come to die on the cross in place of our sins than we would have to pay the penalty for our own transgressions. But the wages of sin are death; the result of separation from Christ, the very tree of life, is anti-life. So Christ died for us. Christ bore the weight that we could not, even though He need not, to do what we would not. That Word, that Logos, speaks to us now through the power of the scriptures and the plain teaching of our hearts and nature. That's why we cannot escape that light, why every man sees the light, because God shows it to us regardless of whether or not we wish to see."

The faint sound of distant church bells interrupted Mo's monologue. He left his chair and walked to the open window. Moses smiled as he saw the old stone church in the distance. It looked like a classic renaissance church with a slate roof and stained glass windows. Great doors marked the entrance and flying buttresses flanked the sides. An ancient graveyard populated the grounds with stone angels and saints. It looked like a small cathedral without the gargoyles.

Mo chuckled. "You know my friends tell me that I'm part of the wrong denomination. I've always wanted to preach in a cathedral. The way stone echoes back the sound is so majestic. It treats the word of God with the reverence that belongs to Him. Especially when you really get a rhythm going...there's nothing quite like it. But I'm afraid that's for far richer Christians. My church can barely afford a building, let alone a medieval castle." Mo breathed in the fresh evening air as he stood by the window. It had been almost a full day since the accident. Now the sun outside was hanging low, and after hours oscillating between preaching and reading out loud his voice was feeling hoarse. Still, better to speak when there were ears to possibly hear than waste words when there was no one left to listen.

But Mo was no longer thinking about preaching.

Instead his mind had wandered back in time. "I used to have a cathedral. It was all mine. Yep, that's right. Mr. poor not-a-dollar-in-his-pocket me had his very own cathedral. My wife knew how much I wanted to preach in one of those buildings, so she gave me a gift one day when we took a trip to the shore. Her parents owned a quaint little summer house and we would go down there and just relax. I remember how much she used to love to swim, but that day she didn't swim at all. No, she spent the better part of the afternoon working on this sand castle behind one of the columns by the pier. She chased me away every time I took a break from fishing and snuck up, trying to get a good look at it. Well, near the end of the day, about when the sun was giving out, she finally let me see what she had been working on.

And low and behold, there was my cathedral. It had flying buttresses and a big door and pretty much everything you could ask for besides a roof. I guess she couldn't find a way to make a roof out of sand. So I stepped over the wall and started to give my first, and to this day my only, sermon in a cathedral. At the beginning I was just having a little fun, but she started laughing so hard that I just kept going. I summoned my most powerful, over dramatic preacher voice. For a moment I felt like Billy Graham and Charles Spurgeon had poured their spirits into my soul. My voice boomed as I waved my hands about in overly dramatic motions. The problem was, she had been working on this thing for so long that now the tide was coming in, and a great wave drenched my cathedral and sent icy cold water up my leg. Suddenly my voice screeched. We both looked at each other and burst out laughing.

Anyway, somewhere in the course of that I'm sure there's a lesson... How about this? The Word of God is so powerful that man cannot restrain it. We try to quarantine it in the great halls of stone, but it pervades through all our imaginary boundaries and runs through all that there is and ever could be." Moses smiled again. "Or maybe I'm just still bitter that my cathedral is gone." The preacher kept staring at the ancient church, enjoying both its sound and the memories it granted.

Chapter 6 – God is Word

Contrary to traditional constructions of natural theology which envision properly basic beliefs as self-autonomous, God, as a being with independent existence, provides the only successful a priori synthetic absolute which can solve the problem of the one and the many via bridging the universal and particular, and thereby satisfy the preconditions of rationality while bypassing the pitfalls associated with foundationalism.

Paul stared dumbly at the first sentence in his brother's senior thesis. In theory, the phrase was written in English. "Dude, the next time I ask to borrow your laptop warn me about the booby traps."

James put down the sketch pad on which he had been drawing a pastel picture of a sunrise looking over the beach. He walked over to the laptop. "Oh, that? Yeah, that's sounds a little complex, but it's actually pretty simple."

Paul stared at his brother the same way he had

years ago when they were kids and the older boy had told him that escargot tasted good. "Right, yeah, simple; only five unintelligible words per sentence," said Paul, sitting in the chair closest to the laptop.

James fired back, "Dude, you can't complain about big words and use 'unintelligible' in the same sentence." Paul couldn't help but smirk. "Ya know, you could write really well if you applied yourself. You skated by Honors English while barely staying awake in class and still got A's."

Paul spun around in his chair. "Now YOU James, of all people, have no right to pick on anyone for slacking off in high school. I remember back in the day you'd hook up with more girls than open books on any given weekend, even before finals, and still managed to tick off everybody else by finishing in the class' top 10. They use to call you 'King James' cause of all the queens at your disposal...and you were the King!"

Paul glanced around his brother's dorm room. The place was different then where he had stayed four years ago. There were no more posters of models in bikinis, no more stashes of hard liquor in the closet, no more beautiful college woman popping their head in every other hour asking James what he was going to do that night, and there certainly was no more crashing frat parties or clubbing. Paul shook his head. "Now you'd rather read a King James...for like, six hours at a time."

Now it was James' turn to lean back in his chair and glance around the room. The place had changed quite a bit. When he was first looking at colleges he knew he wanted to go to some place with a solid reputation. The school needed to have a distinguished history of frats, sororities, toga parties, and other such activities. This was why he chose such a large state school. It's hard for anyone to know your business when you're just another face in the crowd. More importantly, there are always more fish in the sea. Unlike high school where the ramifications of cheating on a girl meant that you had to work twice as hard to get the next, college was a whole different world.

"You know Paul, you're right. When I first showed up here, I never anticipated myself writing something like that. My attitude was summed up by my, 'So many girls, so little time' t-shirt."

Paul interjected. "Speaking of which, where is that thing? If you're never going to wear it I'd like it."

James grinned. "Sorry man, I threw it out with my sports illustrated swim suit posters." Paul sighed. "I know it must seem crazy, but it's well worth it." Paul's expression made James feel like he was escargot. "No Paul, really, this is so much better."

Paul jerked his hands in exasperation. "This!? This is better!? Dude, I remember the best vacation of my life was coming up here to visit you homecoming weekend. Do you know how hard it is for a high school sophomore to land college sorority girls? Well, I guess you did but now I think you forgot. But yeah, that was me, for the whole weekend. And you had that too. You were captain of the football team back in high school. Now, you're captain of the mock trial team! You spend so much time in LSAT books I think you actually enjoy that stuff."

James laughed. "Okay, let's get something straight. I will NEVER enjoy the law school admissions test! But I've already been accepted into my top school, so I don't need to worry about that God forsaken test ever again."

Paul shook his head. "So the next step is the bar, and I'm not talking about the fun kind with booze and babes."

James leaned forward. "See now its clever statements with alliteration and double meanings like that which make me say you have a lot, and I mean A LOT, of natural talent. It took me six months to hit the top ninetieth percentile on the LSAT, but you could probably reach that in half the time with half the effort. You know though, it's really not about that prestige stuff. I didn't change because I wanted to go to law school. Working hard is more a result than the cause. No, the thing that really changed everything was Jesus." Paul ran his fingers through his hair in frustration and braced himself for the coming onslaught.

"You spend your whole life looking for something that's going to make you happy. Everybody does it. They're after something worth living for. They're after that certain something that's missing from all our lives. I used to try to fill it anyway I could. I would search for money and sex; they both made me feel like I had power and entertained me. Here, where we are so blessed, it's extremely easy to lose oneself in an endless stream of entertainment. Everything I had at my disposal was redirected towards a hedonistic search for pleasure. But the pleasure never satisfied for more than a moment. As soon as the high ended I always wanted another. As soon as the surge of adrenaline faded I looked for a new excitement.

You know the Bible talks about a woman like that. She was the kind of gal you'd like; definitely willing to put out. She'd been with a ton of guys, but anyway when Jesus met her He told her that only He could give her what she was looking for. Only He could be that living water that would truly quench her thirst and give her the free gift of grace. And He was right. I wake up every morning knowing that there's a purpose for my life.

There's a meaning behind what I'm here to do. I'm supposed to do exactly what Jesus told Nicodemus when he asked the Lord what he must do to be saved. Jesus told him two things. He needed to love the Lord thy God, and Love thy neighbor as thyself. Or think about it like this; He needed to do good for the sake of doing good, whether that be the expansion of beauty (James gestured with his left hand to a brightly colored painting of a cottage on the wall that use to be covered by a super model), the propagation of knowledge (James gestured towards a rack of books with his right hand), or (extending both hands outward) building great works that soar into the sky like this ten story structure. But equally important, we need to do all this in relation with one another. Creation was never meant to be in isolation from the Creator, man was never meant to be in isolation from woman, and people were never meant to be in isolation from nature."

The two sat in silence for several minutes before Paul finally spoke. "I still don't get it. Alright, I can see the whole beautiful world thing. It makes you feel special to see all of reality in conjunction with yourself. Cool. It got you into a top notch law school with a scholarship. You'll graduate, make good money, find a pretty wife, and go have a little house on the prairie existence in the 21st century. But come on! Do you really expect me to believe that church is better than what you had? You were the man! This type of life is alright if you're the nerd in the back of the class with glasses and a toothpick for a body, but you can do better."

Paul walked over to his brother, and placed his arm around the older man's shoulders. "It's been a couple years now but tell me if this rings a bell." Paul cleared his throat and said mockingly. " 'Well, Paul, this is your first club experience. Your fake ID got you past security so here's your chance to take advantage of a golden opportunity. Now I want you to first feel out the situation. Half the battle of landing a big catch is knowing where the fish are biting. Don't waste your time with girls who are already spending most of the night dancing with one guy. Their boyfriends are here, and even if you can break up a couple it's not worth the trouble. Instead, look for a girl on the outskirts of a group. Women rarely come to these places alone, so you will have to divide and conquer. You can't seduce a whole pack, but you can handle one or two at a time.

" 'Ideally you want to go for two girls who are dancing with each other. They'll feel confident since there's a couple of them, but they don't have enough numbers to make things unwieldy. This will let you move in and pull off some good moves. They'll get excited, dance back, and hopefully you can land a two for one.

" 'Just remember this life lesson until the day you die. You, me, these babes, all of us, we're just mammals. Don't listen to that stuff you hear about restraint and responsibility. What matters tonight is that you are an animal, and here is your prey. This dancing is just the human version of a mating ritual. There is nothing artistic or fancy about it. Just do it well and you will command the attention of sleek, sexy ladies. They will give you whatever you want as long as you play the game of life based on the rules that nature gave us, because they're just animals too. And whatever you do, never be ashamed of what you are. So go forth and conquer, and tomorrow we'll celebrate over some booze.'

"I believe right about then the music started blasting some song about being an animal. Then you slapped my back and I jumped in the rodeo. By the time the night was over, I had gone for quite a number of wild rides and I distinctly remember you keeping your promise to your underage brother with a ton of hard liquor the next night."

James shook his head. "You actually remember that 'how-to-rule-the-club' speech I gave you all those years ago?" His brother's raised eyebrows told him that was a stupid question.

Paul sweetly smiled in the most sarcastic way possible. "Oh dearly beloved brother, just because thou hath lost thy wayeth and left the narrow path to the promised land dost not mean all men have become boys." Paul sighed and returned to his seat.

James smiled. "You know Paul, God really is a synthetic a priori."

Paul wheeled back in his chair, placed his feet on the desk, and rolled his eyes as he said, "Alright Plato, what the heck is a synthetic a priori?"

James' grin looked like it would crack his face if it grew any larger. "So a long time ago on a continent kind of faraway there was a Scotsman by the name of Hume. He was a big, rolly-polly Santa Clause kinda guy. Only replace the jolly demeanor with a nasty habit of assaulting people's faith in God and, for that matter, any other kind of knowledge. Hume was trying to build an epistemology..."

"An e-pis-te what?"

"An epistemology. A theory of knowledge. So he was trying to figure out how you know what you know: Can you trust your senses? Or are rational concepts alone a guide to truth? Or, is knowledge something that comes from a combination of things? And does intuition have any validity? All that stuff counts as epistemology.

"So anyway, he breaks things down into two

generic categories that people usually think in. He talks about the 'analytic' and the 'synthetic'. The analytic is the stuff that defines itself. So 'triangles have three sides' is an analytic statement. It follows from the concept of a triangle that it must have three sides. You can't imagine a triangle with four sides, because that would by definition be a rectangle.

"And the synthetic is that which basically combines information from the senses. So like, say I'm looking at a blue triangle. Is it self-defining that triangles are blue? No. Not at all. But I know it's blue because I see it. So triangles have three sides is a self-defining analytic statement, while that triangle is blue is a sensory based synthetic statement."

Paul regretted his decision to let his brother get started. Now that the man was well underway, there was little he could do but let the engine run out of oil. Still, if nothing else this would at least get the God stuff out of the way sooner rather than later. If all went well, then half an hour wasted on God would then clear the way for a couple man movies or sports; at least Jesus hadn't killed James' love of football. "Now, there are two other categories that he's working with."

"Wait James. So, you're telling me that the

analytic concept thing, and the synthetic experience thing is not enough?"

The older boy smiled. "I think you can handle four new words. So yeah, the other two are 'a priori' and 'a posteriori'. A priori is before or without experience, and a posteriori is after experience. For Hume, they're more or less what we just talked about. In regard to analytic knowledge, triangles having three sides is a priori, or something you can know even if you've never seen a triangle. Kinda like if you told me we're going to call a shape with a billion sides a superplex. I can understand what you're talking about even if I've never seen such a shape and could not imagine drawing it. And a posteriori knowledge is something like, 'Oh look, I see a red triangle. There must be a red triangle.' Tracking so far?"

Paul didn't really care, but figured it was dangerous to stop his brother now. The man had probably poured hundreds of hours into this stuff and would not find another soul willing to hear him out for weeks, so what the heck, why not listen? He could cleanse his brain with video games when he got home. "Yeah, I get it. Analytic and a priori means a concept, and synthetic and a posteriori means an experience.

Can't imagine why I would want it, but I get it."

James was now so close to the edge of his seat that Paul thought he was going to fall off. "Okay, so rolly-polly Scottish Santa, a.k.a. Hume, with his bad attitude runs into a problem. He basically has this system where on the one hand the analytic equals a priori which equals self-defining, and on the other the synthetic equals a posteriori which is based on combining knowledge from senses and stuff. But where do you put cause and effect?

"Suppose we're playing pool and I'm beating you because of course, I'm me and you're you." Paul folded his arms and tried to look annoyed, but his brother continued as if nothing odd had been said. "Now this is pool so we're probably playing at a bar and there're probably a couple hotties at the place. I figured I would throw them in just to keep your attention."

Paul laughed. "Ya know, so far that's the most interesting thing you've said."

The volume of James' voice raised as he exclaimed, "Focus. Focus! FOCUS! Even in thought experiments you can't keep your mind off pretty ladies." Paul took his feet off the desk and was about to protest, but his brother beat him to the chase. "So now the pretty ladies are trying to distract me from my game but I'm too cool for them. The one is wearing a t-shirt with 'King' written on it while the other's says 'James'."

Paul finally interjected, "Okay, what do the girls have to do with anything?"

James beamed while bringing his hands together and bowing in an oriental fashion. "Oh, yes young padawan. You are learning. You may be a philosopher yet." Paul snatched an eraser from off the desk and chucked it at his brother, who easily batted it away with the back of his hand and pressed on. "So anyway, you, in an effort to learn from my mad skills, watch me smack a red pool ball into a blue one. What can you deduce? Well, you know what a sphere is because it's a self-defining concept like any other conceptual idea from geometry. The ball falls into the same category as the triangle. You also know their respective colors because hey, you're looking at them. But can you say that the motion of the red ball caused the blue one to move?"

Paul scratched his head. "Yes?"

In one terribly over dramatic motion James stood raising his arm emphatically and declared, "No!"

Paul had just put his feet back on the desk and the unexpected motion nearly toppled him over. James continued on unabated and spoke with increasing speed as he began pacing back and forth. "You never actually saw cause and effect. You see, you can know the colors of the balls by experience, by the synthetic and the a posteriori, and you can know what a ball is, because you know the definition of a three dimensional circle via the analytic a.k.a. a priori, but you neither actually 'saw' cause and effect, nor is it self-defining that the red ball caused the blue one to move. Now given...."

Paul recovered from his near topple and starred at his brother. "Dude! I totally get it!"

James stopped mid-sentence with his mouth hanging open. After a long moment he asked, "You do?"

Paul smiled. "Yeah man, you were a party animal and you gave it all up for this. I understand now why you did it. Somewhere in the midst of all that drugs, sex, and rock and roll you smoked one to many of ONLY GOD-KNOWS-WHAT and were reduced to babbling madness. Terribly sad, but at least I understand. Note to self, lay off the hard stuff, you never know who you might let inside your head."

James placed his hands on his hips and took a deep breath. "I try educating you with the great insights of universally recognized geniuses and this is the thanks I get."

Paul, like his brother a moment ago, brought his hands together and bowed in an oriental fashion. "Forgive me master Obi-Wan Kenobi. Please share your enlightenment with me." James began pacing again, although this time his movements were far slower. It would take another long, uninterrupted stream of sentences before he built up a comparable rhythm again.

"So Hume winds up as a skeptic who can't even believe that cause and effect works. Yeah, he counters the design argument for the existence of God, but he also kills our ability to trust any kind of science whatsoever like an innocent man under the chopping block of an allegedly enlightened guillotine... kind of like what actually happened during the 'humanistic' French Revolution."

Paul responded. "First off I thought you said slayer Santa was Scottish, but leaving that aside, you really get excited over this whole doom and despair thing. Is that part of the sadomasochist ban on fun? Is there no hope that the sleeping playboy living deep within my brother's mind will ever awaken and see the light?"

James laughed. "No brother. I was blind, but now I see. But anyway I'm not finished. You see, then came Immanuel...and this time I am not talking about Jesus. No, then came Immanuel Kant. Kant was like an innocent, sleeping German baby that was roused from rest by the sound of slaying sanity in the Scottish Hume head."

Paul motioned to the stack of books next to James' desk. Not one of them was less than 700 pages. "It sure looks like slayer Santa killed sanity." On James next pass he swung the computer chair around, sent Paul twirling, and almost tipped his brother over again before he could firmly plant his feet.

"Kant recognized that some things are neither self-defining nor observed, but still a necessary presupposition for the other two categories to operate within. Take space. One does not directly 'see' space. You might see things in space, but you don't actually see space. Nor is space self-defining. I don't know space as some obvious, self-evident truth the way I might know that triangles have three sides. But how could I make sense out of a red ball unless I had a concept of space?

"To put it in previous terms, space is a synthetic a priori. It's something that's integrated with the sense experience, but it's also before or independent of that experience. It's the presupposition of reason. It's the thing that makes the rationality intelligible. Kant builds a category for cause and effect to work in by combining Hume's two types of categories, saves reason, and strikes back against Hume's skepticism. Or, our sleeping German baby levels a smack down suplex on slayer Santa." Paul slowly registered the waves of abstract information coming at him in between his brother's ridiculous mental pictures. James seemed really excited by this, but it all seemed so pointless to Paul.

"Why don't you just say you can infer that the red ball caused the blue ball to move?"

James' face lit up like a Christmas tree as his speech and pacing quickened. "Oh, yes, fantastic! This actually gets into a problem that Kant couldn't solve. So why not just make an inference and move on, right? Well, take an object." James grabbed a tennis ball from off his shelf. "If I drop this ball what will the ball do?"

"Ah...it will fall?"

James let the ball drop and sure enough it hit the floor. He caught it and repeated the process without breaking his stride. "We all think that's so simple. We watch balls drop, then infer that whenever you were to drop a ball anywhere, anytime, it would fall. But hold on there, how many objects exist in the universe? Billions upon trillions, right? And we want to infer some sort of universal law of gravity that will apply across the board, right? We want to say that based off our extremely limited experience we can infer that this thing called gravity is always going to pull an object down, that all balls and rocks and so on are going to drop. But what justification do we have to say that?

"Suppose I saw an Asian man cut me off on the highway. Three months later another Asian man did the same thing. If I inferred from this that all Asians were bad drivers you would rightly call me a bigot. It's ridiculous to say that based on such limited experience. But yet, I would have more justification to say all Asians are bad drivers then I would saying that gravity works, based on the fact that I have seen a couple Asian drivers out of millions of such people, as opposed to the much more vast gulf between the number of objects I've seen fall and the number of objects which are supposedly affected by gravity.

"So now we're right back to the utter collapse of rationality. Without the ability to make warranted inferences from individual events to universal laws of science, and for that matter common sense, can't operate. You'd have to be an infinite being, you'd have to know everything and observe everything, or at least know and observe a lot more than what one measly person is going to in a life time, in order to make probability work."

"Dude, you need to spit out the red pill. Climb out of the rabbit whole Mr. Anderson and leave the matrix so you can tap another Alice. And while you are at it you should spit out any other drugs, and your pool balls, and the rest of your philosophy, and get back to reality. Balls drop because balls drop."

"Balls do drop" James said. And you can connect the many instances of something happening, or what we like to call the particulars, to single rules, or what we like to call universals. Probability does work, and we can make that inference from the many to the one. But the reason why we can do it is because there's an infinite being out there. There's a being which upholds the rationality of the universe. If we will trust that God maintains the order and rationality of the cosmos, then making an inference makes sense. I can say that objects are going to keep on dropping the way they always have because I trust that the great Logos who created the universe through the power of His Word, who sustains that universe, will continue to do so. If I start my thinking there, then the skepticism that plagues the inquisitive mind melts away as God breaths life back into common sense."

"...So... what?"

"So what? SO *WHAT!* So God is a synthetic a priori! So God is the precondition of rationality! So first asserting God makes sense out of what otherwise would be a very disjointed and impossible to understand universe. The Logos makes sense out of life the same way space makes sense out of an object. You can't see either of them, but you know they're there, because without them, what you do see can't make sense. If I start with God, I get to inference. If I start with God I get to science. Heck, if I start with God

I get to ethics and truth and beauty. But, if I start without God I wind up where so many atheists have wound up: skepticism that can't make sense out of a whole world filled with order and beauty. The immediate object only makes sense in light of the transcendent. If God is not holding up reality, then the apex of the pyramid comes crashing down as knowledge gets a black eye and I am stuck with some French existentialism..."

"French philosophy...so like that, 'I think therefore I am' guy right?"

"Well Descartes was a French philosopher, and one of a number of very good ones, but you're a couple centuries too early."

"Oh...wait! Are you talking about that dooer dude?"

"What? Oh you mean Herman Dooyeweerd. Um, well kinda, except he was Dutch. Besides, he is more the next chapter in the book I'm writing. Right now what I am explaining is more presuppositionalism, which after Dutch beginnings, was largely developed and refined in America."

Paul shook his head. "Can't we just pick up a couple French chicks and move on? They have cute accents and believe in gravity. And if you want to, we can even do it in Amsterdam. I hear pot is legal there." James raised his eyes towards the sky and groaned. "Hey, you introduced me to my first French girl. I distinctly remember…"

"Bro, you're killing me. You are injecting hemlock into my veins while forcing me to reread Hegel's *Phenomenology of the Spirit*."

"I take it that's bad."

"Paul! Get outside of your own head and wake up! There is an entire world of truth out there. Reality is an ordered, logical, masterpiece. You can't get your mind out of the gutter long enough to wipe away the filthy sewage and smell the fresh air of the God breathed spirit."

Paul had grown tired of the mental gymnastics. He knew it was time to connect the conversation back to something concrete. But how could one do that with an ivory tower, head-in-the-clouds philosopher? Paul had an idea.

"James, remember that movie *Cast Away*? Remember when Tom Hank's character, the Fed Ex worker, gets stuck on that tropical island all by himself for four years and he has to learn all kinds of skills that a modern man would never bother to learn. He figures out how to find food, shelter, and all the other bare essentials.

"And yet, that's not enough. The cast away also has an insatiable desire to anthropomorphize his environment. He incessantly draws pictures of his former love all over the island he is trapped on, can't help but talk to himself, and befriends a volleyball that he appropriately names Wilson. He has no one to love, and no one to love him. So he creates an imaginary friend and hopes that maybe one day somebody will rescue him.

"Remember when he sets sail and tries to find his way back to civilization. After a great storm, his raft is badly damaged and Wilson begins to float away. He frantically swims after it while crying out for his old friend. The whole scene is extremely powerful but ultimately Wilson is still just a lifeless volleyball with a stupid smiley face drawn on it.

"James, your God is just a smiley face drawn on a cross. You took something as brutal and random as our world and gave it a happy target to shoot for. On the one hand, it's understandable, even admirable. Its pragmatic value cannot be overestimated. There's a reason why religion in one form or another has evolved in every human culture. Religion, despite the fact that on its face value provides no advantage at best, and wastes significant resources at worst, does fulfill the nagging psychological needs of its adherents. However, no matter how much love you may have for your God, no matter how badly you might need answers to the questions that pretending he is there allows you to answer, he is still just a myth you created to solve a problem that your own, frail human nature gave you. Your God gives you two things: false hope for the future and pretend answers about the past.

"This is not necessarily a weakness. The price of consciousness is the need to delude ourselves in one way or another. For some people that involves illusions of grandeur. For others that means pretending life is satisfying when in actuality your marriage is dying and your livelihood is failing. For you that means pretending there is an answer machine called God that grants purpose when really, you have none. But in reality that no more answers your questions and gives you a savior then calling a volleyball Wilson gives a lonely man a friend."

James had sat patiently and absorbed every

word his younger brother had said. This was different. Usually these conversations with Paul were very tense. He had seen his brother walk away from the kitchen table rather than listen to their parents discuss something from scripture. James had tried to convince Paul to at least read a couple books on the subject, but it felt like amputating a limb without drugs. At least this time he had Paul talking in a calm voice. James lifted his eyes toward heaven as a prayer for wisdom graced his mind, and then the rebuttal began.

"Your argument is clever, but it sidesteps much of my reasoning. I give you a point by point explanation of how belief in God provides a better foundation for rationality, to which you retort by saying I merely use God to lay my burning questions to rest. First, it should be noted that you never actually countered my argument per se; all you did was try to give a psychological explanation for why I advanced my argument in the first place. But pushing that aside for one moment, your counterargument is a double-edged sword that can just as easily cut off your own head.

"Think about it; doesn't atheism fulfill a psychological need? What if you came to believe in the sort of God I am talking about? What if you came to believe in a personal God that wants a relationship with you and creates a standard of righteousness outside of yourself? If you believed in this sort of God, you would have to radically alter your life. You would need to stop with the drugs, sex, and rock and roll, and instead pursue the difficult, disciplined life of the pious. It is easier for you to find any way to avoid Christianity.

"At first you'll mock it. After all, if it's ridiculous then you don't need to believe it. But when you come across a well-reasoned defense of God, then you fall back on a pseudo-psychological analysis that is really just an ad hominem, personal attack dressed up in scientific-sounding language. The skeptic can call God a coping mechanism if he wants, but really, atheism is just a way of coping with a guilty conscious that lets someone keep on sinning with minimal interference.

"Both of our worldviews allow us to get through the day, but there are two fundamental differences between them. First off, mine provides a functional explanation for why reason works. Mine gives me a rational starting point from which to begin my thinking. But aside from that, my goal-directed process adds a beauty to reality that yours cannot. Let's assume we both use coping mechanisms. Well yours lets you fill your life with cheap thrills, but mine challenges me to be a better person and change the world. Even if I strip away everything else, and just compare our 'coping mechanisms', my Christ still beats your hedonism." And with a smug smile, James flopped down in his chair.

Paul looked around the room and saw what his brother had become. It was quite ironic. Most "good kids" went to college and came back bad. They were solid students who got decent grades and didn't drink or smoke or have rampant sex. Then you put them in a consequence-free environment where the only moral boundaries are provided by their peers while the professors hacked away at any vestige of tradition still living in their heads and suddenly it was freshman gone wild.

But James slacked off in high school and slept with half the pretty cheerleaders. Now, here he was in college, in the prime of his life, and he had just turned his back on all of it. His dorm was crammed with too many books and no babes. The shelves were stuffed with boring titles like *Critique of Pure Reason,*

Who is God?

Meditations, Summa Theologica, Plato's Republic, and
the list went on. The books on his desk and the piles
around it that apparently had helped him write this
tome of a senior thesis covered things like natural
theology, epistemology, metaphysics, logic, and a ton
of other topics that normal people did not care about.
Right now even a pale, skinny nerd had a higher
probability of getting laid than James. At least the
nerd would probably hook up with some anime chick
at a role playing convention or something. James, on
the other hand, was too deep into his books to really
see beyond them. But at least the guy was happy.

"Look, Paul. I know this all seems abstract. But
it really does make sense. It really makes sense out of
everything. I've seen a lot of smart people tell me flat
out that they can't see any justification for ethics. That
after taking some ethics classes they can't see why
there's any right or wrong, and after taking some
epistemology classes they can't see how they could
know anything, and after taking some metaphysics
classes they can't see how anything could be true. The
greatest geniuses in history have time and time again
come up against the deep questions and left
discouraged and broken; brilliant minds literally

unable to confidently put two and two together. But it need not be like that. They get no conclusions because they won't start with the right presupposition. Start with God and life will matter, start with the Logos and words have meaning..."

....

In the beginning was the Word, and the Word was with God, and the Word was God. The same was in the beginning with God. All things were made by him; and without him was not any thing made that was made.

Mo finished reading the opening lines in the first chapter of John's gospel. "So you see Paul, Jesus is the Word, or as the Greek says, the 'Logos'. It's interesting that 'logos' is where we get the English word 'logic' from. John could have just as easily used the other Greek word for 'word' there. But he didn't, because Christ is not here to confuse. After all, God is not the author of confusion. No, God is the author of a revelation. God self-identifies as Logos, because God is the Word that reveals Himself. We could never find answers in this creation without God, but through Him this place starts to make sense.

"This is a lot like Romans when it tells us... well

hold on one second and let me flip to it.

> For therein is the righteousness of God revealed from faith to faith: as it is written, The just shall live by faith. For the wrath of God is revealed from heaven against all ungodliness and unrighteousness of men, who hold the truth in unrighteousness; Because that which may be known of God is manifest in them; for God hath shewed it unto them. For the invisible things of him from the creation of the world are clearly seen, being understood by the things that are made, even his eternal power and Godhead; so that they are without excuse: Because that, when they knew God, they glorified him not as God, neither were thankful; but became vain in their imaginations, and their foolish heart was darkened. Professing themselves to be wise, they became fools, And changed the glory of the incorruptible God into an image made like to corruptible man, and to birds, and four-footed beasts, and creeping things.

"Notice a couple things here. The glory of God, even down to His eternal power and Godhead, is clearly seen. Paul, there's not one spec of this universe over which Christ does not exert His rightful sovereignty. God is Lord over all, so much so that if you reject God then very quickly reality just doesn't make sense anymore. Just as the heavens declare the glory of God, that which denies the glory of God can only declare babel. That's why Christ is Logos, not mere mythos. And that's why God created through the Logos. The logic of this world is a word that is there to tell us about THE WORD.

"It saddens me to think of our fallen world. I remember my brother-in-law. He was a nice guy, incredibly talented. I can't count how many times he beat me in basketball and chess, and he was one of the funniest men I ever met. One thing in particular sticks in my mind when I think about him though: He used to love Frank Sinatra, and could sing his songs so well you almost couldn't tell the difference between him and the record. But anyway, he lived by that one Sinatra song that says, 'I did it my way.' That's what this guy wanted to do with his life. He wanted to live his own life, make his own decisions, and be the master of his own autonomy. The thought of submitting to a higher power than himself and following someone else's plan for his life was repulsive.

"Boy he used to drive my Dad crazy! My old man was a preacher, too. Hence how I got a name like Moses, and a couple brothers named Abraham and Joseph, and a sister named Charity. But anyway, that's why my brother-in-law went where he wanted to go, purchased what he wanted to purchase, and lived the ideal life by modern standards. He owned a big house, multiple cars, and went on exotic vacations. And he kept at it, kept doing things his way until the day he died. He ignored all my preaching for decades and then he finally figured out that everything he held dear wasn't worth it.

"I remember talking to him on his death bed. By that point, his handsome features had shriveled up, and his silky voice had turned as rough as sand paper. And he told me that he felt like nothing he had done in life really mattered. Nothing he had purchased or built was really going to last. To a large extent it was true. He couldn't take any of his expensive toys to heaven, and he had always put more time into the love of money than people or causes. Sadly, even in his pain I still don't think he ever made his peace with God.

"We can all feel the Spirit moving deep within us. We intuitively know that there is so much more to live for and that absolutes are there regardless of whether or not we want to pretend otherwise. The problem is, we ignore the gentle embrace of God so we can pursue vain pleasures instead of His love. We think breaking commandments is more fun than obeying them, but when we ignore God we don't break His laws. Instead, we use His laws to break ourselves.

"Just look at your predicament. I don't even know if you can hear me. I met you less than 24 hours ago. I've been preaching to you for hours now without as much as a bat of an eyelash. How did you wind up with broken bones and enough drugs in your system to make a chemistry lab jealous? It's because you missed the beauty of all this. You missed the point behind why we are here. You thought that life was about doing your own thing. You bought the lie that drugs, sex, and rock and roll were better than anything God had to offer. And now look at you. You're right where my brother-in-law was; a life that was lived without producing anything to show for it.

"You didn't see the Logos that lives in the logic, which made you deaf to the Word being sung by the song of creation, from the sparkle in a pretty girl's eyes to the light of a distant star. But it doesn't have to be this way. I've seen people just like you, people who teetered on the edge of oblivion without any hope for what comes next. And I've seen them put their faith in something greater than themselves and trust that the rationality which binds the fabric of our world together is not a cold machine, but a benevolent mind with a warm smile."

Chapter 7 – God is a Scientist

The peaceful skies retreated before the oncoming tempest. Low storm clouds tumbled over each other, barreling forward in a turbulent race. They were dark and foreboding, and with them sailed a small lake on the verge of breaking through its heavenly seal. The moment they did great showers would cascade towards earth like a legion of tiny, wet lightning bolts. Huge arcs of electricity accompanied the powerful clouds and sent vibrations through one's bones. Paul watched dozens of people fleeing before the encroaching spectacle, all save one. Despite the intimidating violence of the approaching storm he stood his ground. Dozens rushed past, all heading for cover in a series of brick buildings a few hundred yards off, but this man stoically stared directly into the clouds.

Paul was not sure what to do. He wanted to turn tail and run like the sensible people around him, but something about this man's peculiar actions made Paul want to talk to him. What was he doing? Was he insane? Didn't he care if he was struck by lightning? Was he trying to mock God straight to the deity's face? Paul decided that discretion was the better part of valor, and headed for cover with the rest of the sheep. But the man stood. Even as the wind became so fierce that it blew his hair and garments straight back with such vigor, Paul knew the loner must be struggling to hold his ground, but the man held firm. As Paul reached the thick metal doors and brown walls of the building which everyone was heading to, the rain swept over the man.

Paul thought that surely the torrent would make him reconsider, but instead of turning his back to the storm the man slowly removed his scarlet jacket. He then lifted his arms and head towards the sky. The water was pelting him directly in the face while his outstretched arms only made him more susceptible to the wind. Even his fingers stretched as if to absorb every morsel of energy that nature could dispense. Yet, the figure remained relaxed with his eyes closed and his body exposed. First one minute, then two, three, five, and ten, and eventually thirty passed. All those behind the safety of the concrete, metal, and glass marveled at the fool. Why subject himself to such obvious discomfort? Slowly the power of the storm subsided, and after the weather had done its worst, the man retrieved his jacket, turned, and began to walk towards the same metal doors that the others had fled to.

Paul overheard the comments people were saying. "What a shame that the track meet was rained out; I thought the Cardinals were gonna make a comeback..."

"Wow, that was the weirdest change in the weather I've ever seen. One second it was beautiful out, and the next I was looking around for Noah..."

"That Mr. Weinberg sure is something, ant' he? Standing out there in the storm. He's gotta be nuts..."

Eventually the physics teacher made his way back to the high school where he worked. The man was so absolutely drenched that Paul thought even his blood must be drier than his skin. The room hushed and parted when he entered as everyone either awkwardly looked away or stared. It seemed obvious that they had been talking about him, but Mr. Weinberg didn't care. He walked past everyone, including Paul, without acknowledgment. Paul walked after him half out of the desire to question him, and half out of the eerie feeling that he was supposed to.

The man headed down the long hall, turned the corner, and entered the teacher's lounge. Paul followed. Mr. Weinberg flipped the switch on the room's electric heater, grabbed a roll of paper towels, took a seat, and began drying himself off.

"What were you doing out there?"

The teacher looked up at Paul. The response was matter of fact and nonchalant. "I was talking to God."

Paul was obviously skeptical. Did the man hear voices in his head? Maybe he was crazy. "What did God say?" He scoffed.

Mr. Weinberg smiled. "I would translate if I knew how, but I'm afraid I don't. You'll have to talk to God yourself if you want to know."

"Do you often talk to God?"

"Oh yes, as often as I can. Every day, in fact. Usually I prefer to do it at sunrise or sunset, but thunderstorms are a rare treat. Paul, do you ever talk to God?"

Paul took a step back. "You...you remember me?"

Mr. Weinberg gestured to the chair next to him. "Of course! Your graduation wasn't that long ago. Besides, your dad talks about you all the time."

Paul sat down. "Really? What does he say?"

The physics teacher twitched his head emptying the water out of his ear. "Well, lately he's been pretty worried about you. He seems to think you have a lot of untapped potential. That you could've been a straight A student but skated by with mostly B's and C's, and that you have no real direction. He was very encouraged when your brother started putting his nose in the books and got himself into a top notch law school, but he's afraid you might fall through the cracks and just spend the rest of your life meandering from one dead end job to another."

Paul grunted in disapproval. Several things about this teacher unnerved him. For one thing, the man seemed to know a lot about his personal life. Sure, Mr. Weinberg and his father had worked together for years and probably shared a lot over the course of that time. But still, talking to a near stranger who knew your name and personal life was like talking to a critical version of your subconscious. To make matters worse, the man was just downright strange.

Who is God?

He appeared unassuming enough, like a stereotypical science nerd. He was thin and lanky and despite his near six-foot frame he probably weighed no more than 145 pounds. His hair was tangled and unkempt, and a pair of thick glasses hung in his shirt pocket.

Yet the man was unnerving in an unspoken kind of way. Maybe it was just his eccentric manner of not caring what others said about him. Everyone would like to think that they don't need the approval of others around them, but in reality we are social creatures and people who can feel accepted in the face of rejection are rare and usually crazy. What made this man so willing to be looked at cross eyed just so that he could experience something different? But the strangest thing about him was just how comfortable he was talking about God.

Most people keep their beliefs about God private, as they should. This abomination against intellect was an unfortunate state of affairs, a regrettable hold over from a past era in human evolution that was taking longer for natural selection to remove than was preferable. But at least most people kept their weaknesses to themselves. There was nothing more obnoxious than a person who just threw their opinions

---

about God in your face. But this physics teacher had a quiet boldness about his faith that almost matched that Puritan preacher from the red light district who would never shut up.

"You talk a lot about God for a man of science. Didn't your training in knowledge put a damper on your mysticism?"

Mr. Weinberg looked directly into Paul. He studied the younger man like an interesting, albeit familiar, specimen before responding. "Mysticism, at least in the way you are probably imagining it, is blasphemy. If Christ had wanted mysticism He would have appeared as "mythos", not "logos". No, God is not the word of insanity, but rather the essence of rationality."

Paul was quick to retort. "Yeah, that's why you need faith in order to believe in him."

"Define faith." The older man fired back just as quickly.

Paul calculated before responding. This man seemed ready to back up his insane claim. Was this a trick question? No, it couldn't be. Everyone knew what faith was... "Faith is believing in what you have no evidence for, to believe in something without reason."

The physics teacher smiled. "Did you get that definition from the scriptures?" Paul had never read more than a couple pages in the Bible. He couldn't honestly tell the man yes, but was sure the book said something along those lines. Still, Paul decided to play things safe and shake his head no.

"You know, the Bible actually gives a definition of faith. And it's basically the exact opposite of what you just said. According to Hebrews 11:1, 'faith is the substance of things hoped for, the evidence of things not seen'. Now consider that for a moment. Everyone seems to think that the Bible tells us to have blind faith. As Mark Twain use to advocate, 'Faith is believing what you know ain't so.' But when the Bible gives a definition of faith, it doesn't emphasize uncertainty but rather the certainty of faith. It speaks to how the difference between faith and another belief is the addition of hope, *not* the subtraction of evidence. Not to mention the entire book of Proverbs is about wisdom and knowledge and the need to pursue both. Oh, and let's not forget many of the Psalms teach the same thing. And like I said, Jesus is called 'logos', not 'mythos'. If you want to pick on believing something because it's absurd go attack existentialist philosophy, the majority of which comes out of atheism anyway... Kierkegaard notwithstanding."

This struck Paul as backward. Everything Paul had ever heard about faith said there was a joy in believing without reason. "If that's really what the Bible says then how come Christians have always taught the exact opposite? Why did Columbus have to fight the church in the dark ages in order to sail around the supposedly flat earth and..."

The soaking physics teacher burst into laughter. He slapped both his knees, leaned back in his chair, and folded his arms. "Oh yeah? Which Christians? Was it Justin Martyr back in the first century who taught that Christianity was the most rational philosophy? Or how about Augustine, the most influential Christian theologian of his millennium and arguably the most important one of all time? Was his belief that God was the most intelligible of all beings an embrace of irrationality? Or maybe Anselm, the man who said that he believed in order that he might understand.

"Or maybe Aquinas with his systematic *Summa Theologica*, which built on Augustine and Anselm and to this day remains arguably the most systematic philosophy ever written? Was it Erasmus, the greatest scholar of his day and the father of humanism? Or maybe his intellectual disciples in Luther or Calvin? Or what about Jonathan Edwards, probably the greatest American philosopher who ever lived, the spearhead of the first great awakening, and a man so convinced of the rationality of God that he developed an entire philosophy which incorporated the divine mind into literally all of reality? If not them, then why not Abraham Kuyper, prime minster of the Netherlands, creator of a major research university, and defender of a fully God-centered worldview that placed Christ at the foundation of literally every subject? Did he teach this belief because it's absurd?

"Oh, and as far as the so called dark ages and Columbus thing goes, you need to rethink those old wives tales. The church never taught that the earth was flat. Heck, the most popular science textbook on astronomy during the middle ages was titled *Sphere*! The only thing that got Columbus into so much trouble was his miscalculation of the earth's circumference. If it hadn't been for the Americas, which Columbus presumably had no reason to believe existed, he would have died at sea. And during those oh-so-dark ages, we saw the development of integrated stirrups and saddles which made heavy cavalry possible, and new types of harnesses that let farmers replace their oxen with horses. This literally doubled their productivity. They even invented iron horse shoes, as well as mills, mechanical clocks, the suspended compass, and enough other leaps in science to make Europe the most technologically advanced civilization by the rise of scholasticism. All of this happened during the Christian era and well before the fall of Constantinople which created the Renaissance and a new awareness of classical literature. Christendom became the most scientifically sophisticated place on earth well before pagan thought was rediscovered."

Paul stammered. "Well... if you Christians are all about learning and science than why has the church always opposed the university and all that it stands for?"

Mr. Weinberg laughed another good, hearty laugh that showed how much he was enjoying this conversation. "Who do you think built the university? There had been tutors for many millennium, but learning was always a rich man's game. The church made monasteries and abbeys, which opened learning to members of every economic class and both genders. Most of the greatest universities in the world whether they be Harvard, Oxford, or the like, were founded by Christians for the propagation of learning. Do you realize that as we speak the Bible has been translated into over 2,000 languages, and that hundreds of new translations are in the works? Humanity will see worldwide literacy in this century. Do you really think that would have been possible without the Bible producing legions of people willing to give up comfortable lives in lucrative places, only to move half way around the world and spend their entire existence helping those whom they had never met learn to read?

"It's no accident that the rise of science rode the wave of natural theology. That men in droves, whether they be Kepler or Newton or dozens of others, for the first time in history looked out into the natural world and saw a message, a word, that was meant to be read, after they had read the Bible. And after reading the book of books they found the will to read the book of nature; hence why the great works of the scientific revolution often thank God in their prefaces. If you want to find an assault on science, look to those who say we were not designed to understand reality; that the universe cares nothing for man's mind.

"I'll tell you what. Why don't you solve a problem that no atheist I've yet spoken with has been able to get around? You tend to think that reason works, right? That rationality sets up rules that govern this universe, right?"

"Well...yeah...?"

"So if it's mathematically and conceptually impossible for say...a triangle to have four sides, then we can be sure that they don't, right?"

"Yes. What's your point?"

"In a nut shell if it doesn't make sense rationally it can't be true. Everything that exists must be rational?"

Paul rolled his eyes. "Yeah, I believe that Mr. Physics teacher, and so should you. That is unless you teach one thing six days a week and preach another thing come Sunday."

"So the limits of reality are defined by reason, by the conceptually possible?"

"Yes, okay! Things make sense! Science works. Math doesn't take a vacation. And again, what's your point? You're the one who believes in miracles and

thinks those laws of science sometimes don't apply.
What are you suggesting? That it's irrational to be
rational?"

"Oh no, not at all. What I would like to know is
why you think your brain is in a position to place
restrictions on what is possible due to the limitations
of your own mind." Paul's raised his eyebrows in
confusion. Mr. Weinberg continued. "Okay, let's go
back to the triangle with its three sides. You assume
that triangles have to have three sides, right? I mean,
if it had four sides it would by definition be a
rectangle. That seems like a self-defining, necessary
concept and to deny it would require the utter
breakdown of all rationality. So you accept it,
presumably with warrant?"

The strange feeling of deja vu was creeping over
Paul. He was not sure why triangles seemed so
dangerous, but he knew he didn't trust them. "I'm still
not following...?"

"Stay with me just a little longer. Could I say
triangles must have three sides because it is
conceptually impossible for them not to?"

Paul could barely hold back his frustration at
the man's repetitive fascination with the mundane.

"Yes! Who cares!?"

"Presumably monkeys cannot conceive of triangles, yes?"

"What?" Paul threw up his hands.

"Do you think a monkey even knows what a triangle is?" Mr. Weinberg leaned forward as he asked, "You wouldn't say that a monkey can do geometry would you? A monkey could never understand something like the Pythagorean Theorem. Or at the very least, there are many concepts which we humans know to be true that monkeys cannot conceive of?"

"Okay..."

"So why assume that a monkey can define reality based on the limitations of what he can imagine," Mr. Weinberg said as he pointed at Paul. "Ultimately, the distinction between a monkey and a man within an atheistic evolution is only one of degree. Both groups have common ancestors, and we just happened to have evolved a cognitive faculty that is better at processing information than our more dim witted cousins. But there is no definitive difference in kind. Man might not be a monkey per se, but he is limited by the same mindless evolutionary process. If a monkey cannot conceive of all that there is, why should a man?"

Paul stared slack jawed. "Really? You, of all people, given your profession, hand me some creationist garbage? Did you fall asleep in all your classes or do you just arbitrarily ignore science when convenient?" Mr. Weinberg smiled at Paul's insult. It was strange, almost like the man enjoyed the cheap shots. Maybe he really didn't care what other people thought of him.

Mr. Weinberg continued: "You assume my arguments are of a very different stripe than that which I now advance. You seem to believe that I am making some anti-evolution argument that will, if successful, strip you of any hope for a working cosmology and anthropology. Really, my argument is much more sweeping than that. I am not saying that you have utilized incorrect reason. Rather, I claim that you have absolutely no right to use any kind of reason whatsoever. The moment you say a self-defining concept like triangles must have three sides you stop thinking like an atheist and act like a theist."

"That's absurd!" Shouted Paul.

"Oh is it? Under your system life was not designed. There is nothing transcendent about it. Life is a meaningless accident. The universe does not care that you exist, and will not care when you cease to exist. So why would you make the utterly arrogant claim that if you cannot conceive of it than it cannot be true. By what power does your atheism grant you such a divine right? You are not thinking God's thoughts after Him. You are not here to know or comprehend. There is no lawgiver that created children so that they might observe the mind of their maker. You only exist to reproduce. Sex, not knowledge, is the meaning of your life. So even a bare bones, in your face, how on earth could you ever doubt this kind of statement like triangles have three sides is beyond what you could ever justify. Maybe they do and maybe they don't, but either way a limited mind stranded from accessing universal truth will never find out one way or the other."

Paul shook his head in disgust. "That's simple, I know that my mind works because if it didn't I wouldn't survive! It's pretty hard to stay alive if you can't trust that you're looking at food or running from a predator. Or did you never bother to read that great work of science called the *Origin of Species*. It was published in 1859 so I know a 'scientist of your caliber' might have trouble keeping up with such a recent publication."

Mr. Weinberg once again ignored the insult. "There is no law which guaranties whatever is true is necessarily the most pragmatic, unless we beg the question and define truth as pragmatism. Is there an obvious survival advantage to believing in an afterlife in a universe lacking one? According to your system there must have been. Why else would various examples of what you call religion ever evolve? And yet, you claim it is not true. Well, so much for saying that evolution must breed better truth machines."

Paul groaned. "It's called genetic drift, a term I know you're probably not familiar with. Sometimes a particular species evolves not because it is better adapted, but because it just got lucky. If you're the best predator alive, but an asteroid wipes out the climate you need then you're dead and the competition still wins. That's a large part of why our ancestors survived. So did religion necessarily have a survival advantage? Well, maybe it just came about for the same reason why we did: dumb luck. And besides, even if something was useful in the past that doesn't mean it will remain useful in the future."

Mr. Weinberg wore his largest grin yet. "Which all demonstrates my point. Survival of the fittest allows for some measure of a goal directed process without a goal giver, or so the argument runs. However, even under your naturalistic system you still have to deal with dumb luck. Your mind did not get here in order to think. Instead, it only exists to propagate its own genes. This problem is so extensive that you admit much of your own evolution was not directed towards survival. Let's suppose survival of the fittest is your bridge to confidence and shows you your mind is functioning in a way that corresponds to reality. It's the only thing telling you the truth about how the universe works. If so, then the more distance you put between survival of the fittest and your own evolution with things like genetic drift the more problematic your epistemology becomes.

"But even if we ignore the problem of genetic drift, you still have not successfully connected survivability to truth. Think about this. For centuries, people thought that time was a constant. Obviously my time was no different from your time. A second for a physics teacher was the same as a second for a physics student. But then Einstein came along with

Who is God?

$E=MC^2$ and suddenly time was relative. If one object is traveling near the speed of light then it also travels through time faster. A second really doesn't always equal a second. In other words, we found a triangle with four sides.

"Now for a guy like me that's not a problem. I never expected reality to be without its puzzles. After all, is it not the glory of God to hide a thing, and the glory of man to find it? My confidence in the intelligibility of reality lays in my belief that God made the puzzle of creation in order to teach His creation about Himself, not in some arrogant abstract assertion which says if I can't imagine it then it can't be. But if you're basing your knowledge of truth on what is conceptually possible, then the knowledge that even the conceptually impossible might exist is damning.

"There is absolutely no basis for an atheist to begin working in a field like analytic philosophy, mathematics, or physics. There are no sure principles for you to start theorizing from. If seconds are elusive then how can we be sure we understand simple shapes like triangles, let alone complex logical axioms? So even if you had a perfect naturalistic evolutionary history untainted by luck, that was truly a long march towards increasing pragmatic survivability, you would still never find a certain intellectual basis for your thinking."

"Oh, and by the way, I have read that great work of natural theology researched by the then recently graduated seminarian called Charles Darwin. It seems that Darwin, like Newton, did his best science when he was closest to God. But don't become to enamored with good old Chuck. Remember, he said nothing about genetics. We had to wait for an Augustinian monk named Mendel to complete his research at the monastery before science discovered the foundation of biology."

Paul grimaced as Mr. Weinberg stared him down. "That's crazy!?" Spat Paul. "Are we supposed to reject all science because somewhere out there in the great unknown there might be a lurking truth that we have yet to stumble upon? I say we should at least try to find the truth, even if our limitations get in the way."

"Oh heavens! Let us not forsake the acclimation of knowledge. We are to study and exegete the great book of nature just as we do the same for the great book of scripture. And we should do these things because we *can* understand! We can understand that reality makes sense because this is not an accident. The very reason why we're here is to think God's thoughts after Him. When I say something is conceptually impossible, I am not merely a spinoff of a monkey's grandpa. Maybe that's part of how God chose to build us and maybe it isn't. Either way, I am made in the image of a transcendent mind which crafted this extraordinary universe, and I can consequently trust that my mind can eventually master more than hip thrusting. But you on the other hand... you're just an animal, so why should you trust yourself?"

"So you're telling me that without God my mind is little better than that of a monkey."

"Oh hell no! Don't flatter yourself and insult the monkey. Your circumstances are far more dire than that. Without God you are not equivalent to a monkey, but lower than a serpent. At least the monkey knew his place."

Paul wanted to object. He was ticked off now; there was no need to get personal. Besides, he was certain that this could not be true. After all, everyone knew science and religion were supposed to be enemies, right? But this physics teacher knew a thing or two about science and had apparently read some history too. It might be better to attack him from another angle.

Paul smirked as a new question formed in his mind. The hot shot know it all would never be able to tackle this challenge, and would then have to retreat back into the cowardly refuge of blind faith.

"Alright, you say that Christianity is all about adding hope, not subtracting evidence. Apparently, belief in God is supposed to give people a certain sense of meaning and purpose. It's supposed to make people want to study the world and produce beautiful art because the whole thing is designed and ordered and all that. And I guess you also think that it makes sense out of laws of science and mathematics.

"Well, in that case I've got a question for you. God is three in one, right? Three persons and one essence. Now what in your hellish heaven does that mean? Does one and one and one equal one? Or are there three gods? And don't try and wrestle out of this with some comment about God being a mystery. Not after that whole logos speech combined with the atheists are ridiculous because we can't account for triangles or logic thing."

Mr. Weinberg left his chair and headed towards a cabinet on the far side of the room. From there he retrieved a black, leather-bound King James Bible with worn binding and frayed edges. He walked back towards Paul and stood in front of him.

"This is the only time I am going to say this, but in order to get a proper answer I'm afraid we're going to have to keep this book closed...for now. I want you to think back to basic concepts in physics. We talk about matter and energy. A secular naturalist would say that everything in physics is an outworking of these two things, that if it exists then we can explain it as matter and its motion. So with that said, look at this book. Obviously it has matter. We can see the object, we can also touch it, weigh it, measure it, and so on. It has height, width, depth, mass, density, and all the other properties which one would expect in a given object. Do you agree?"

Paul hesitated. He had seen people start off innocent enough with basic statements and then find ways to twist them back towards God before. He was also sure that this was exactly what the physics teacher planned to do. But he couldn't find a place to counter him yet, so Paul nodded in approval and let the teacher continue.

"Good. There's also another property contained within this object. That property is potential energy. The higher I lift this book, the more potential energy it has. The book would hit the ground with more force if I were to let it go while it was elevated over my head than if it were only a few inches off the ground. This potential energy is a measurable property, which can be described with mathematical precision and repeated in scientific experiments. In fact, it's such a basic concept that without it, all physics would come crashing down–no pun intended."

"Ok, how does this show that your god is not a contradiction?" Paul crossed his arms across his chest.

Mr. Weinberg began slowly raising and lowering the book. "As I elevate and then lower this book an invisible but very real property of the object is in flux. Nothing about the book's particles are changing, and the same goes for the floor. So, it seems like in order to explain this object I will need to talk about at least matter and this quantifiable potential energy, right?"

Paul frowned. "Yeah, okay, but what does any of this have to do with the trinity?"

"So it's fair to say that the matter is fully manifest throughout the book. Every part of the book that is this book is also fully integrated with the matter. Likewise, the potential energy is fully manifest throughout this book. Everything that is the book also contains the energy. I cannot explain one apart from the other, and both are fully manifest in the book." The teacher waited a moment to see if Paul would make the connection, but the blank stare on his student's face showed this to be wishful thinking.

"The point of the Trinity is to say that there are three persons in God: Father, Son, and Holy Ghost, right? And these three beings are all one, and yet they are all distinct. You call this a contradiction, but if it's impossible for multiple modalities, perspectives, aspects, or whatever else you want to call them, to exist as fully part of what they are without losing their distinctions then you will fail to explain this book or any other object as well as the triune God. Both the object and the Trinity form a complete whole. And in both cases you have an aspect which is fully integrated with the entirety of the whole, which cannot be separated from any part of it, and yet remains distinct from something else which is also fully a part of the whole. I cannot strip the potential energy from the elevated book, nor can I strip the Ghost from the Father.

"You need to stop thinking about reality as if it were just one giant machine. A part is a piece of something, and yes, the parts do make up much of the whole. But there is something more and just as real, existing in everything and everyone. These additional aspects of a given object manifest themselves throughout each part, without ever becoming reducible to those parts. There is a sense in which reality works according to undeniably mechanically based principles and analogies. However, these parts are not the whole story. You cannot understand something without looking at the parts which make it, but the parts alone will only ever give you a half truth. For the whole truth, you need to understand the relation between every relevant part and aspect.

"And I can press this analogy further. One could move past spatial relations to temporal relations, logical relations, mathematical relations, and on and on. All of reality, both in creation and the Creator, constantly exists in relation. If you want to know who God is, if you want to understand the essential character and being of God, then you need to understand Him in relation. God is an inherently relational being. That's why He, despite being infinite and lacking nothing, chose to create. Namely, so that He could be in relation with another entity outside Himself. That's who God is, and who we should be. In order for you to know who you are, you are going to have to understand who He is, because who you are is defined by your relation to Him."

Paul responded with silence. The physics teacher was once again turning out to be more capable than he expected. Still, as the young man reviewed these arguments one glaring weakness emerged.

"I still don't get it. Your whole religion is based on miracles. Virgins don't get pregnant, men don't walk on water, and people don't raise from the dead. How can you call yourself a man of science, and sit here using reason when convenient, and then go ahead and believe in miracles whenever the Bible calls for something impossible. You'll smash holes in my argument but what of your own desecrations of science. You can't observe miracles in a laboratory. By definition they violate scientific law."

"What is a scientific law?" asked Mr. Weinberg flatly.

Paul stopped to consider. "A scientific law describes an intrinsic property of matter."

Mr. Weinberg nodded. "Not a bad answer... for an atheist. But you will ultimately create more problems than you solve like that. If the law exists in specific examples of matter, in the particulars, then we have no reason to believe that the law is universal or eternal. If matter only drops because the matter we have contacted happens to have a thing called gravity, on what grounds do we assume matter always behaves this way or always will?"

Paul ran his fingers through his hair. "Wait. So you're saying gravity does not have to work even if every object obeys the laws of gravity?"

"That's right. Yes, every object obeys the law of gravity. It does so because the Word of the Lord has ordained that one of the laws upholding His creation is a thing we call gravity. But suppose you took away the law, which is distinct from the objects which it governs. Why would the matter have to keep behaving the way that it does? Matter changes. It ebbs and flows. Laws of science are supposed to be more consistent than that. They are the things that give matter its properties. If matter gave itself these seemingly immaterial, timeless, universal properties then the material would be infusing itself with the immaterial."

Paul took a deep breath as he tried to follow the abstract direction the physics teacher was moving in. "Paul, try chewing on this. Look at a wall. It seems solid, right? Doesn't exactly look like something you would want to try to run through, right? But if I said to you that a concrete wall is empty then I would be closer to the truth then if I said the wall is solid. The wall is made of atoms, and the atoms are mostly made of nothing. The nucleus is ten thousand times smaller than the atom at large. The rest of the atom is mostly just a bunch of empty space. So why can't you run straight through that wall? It's not because there is anything there that is intrinsically solid enough to stop you. You can't run through that wall for the same reason why Mario can't normally run through one of the walls in the Princess' castle. Namely, the rules laid down by the architect say you can't."

Paul scrunched his forehead in bewilderment.

"Okay Paul, bear with me for a moment. Suppose this universe is not the final reality. Suppose that maybe, just maybe, we live in the dream world, or a digital simulation, or whatever else you want to call a world that is somehow less real than something just beyond it. What if the so called laws of science are really nothing more than consistency in God's choices, what if they are just the programing rules that the great programmer laid down when He created this program? If that's the world we live in, then a miracle is no more a violation of the laws of science than a repeatable lab based experiment. If you can come up with a conception of reality without God that makes more sense than my theism then maybe I should revise, but until you do I have no problem harmonizing my miracle bearing theism with all the laws of science. A miracle is just a temporary alteration in the programing code which the master programmer created. Its kind of like entering a cheat code into a video game. Rewriting or suspending the rules is no more a violation of them than their initial writing. In fact, only that miracle bearing theism can explain the greatest miracle of all, namely, the fact that the laws of science are there in the first place. Or as Einstein once said, 'The most incomprehensible thing about the universe is that it is at all comprehensible.'"

There was so much more Paul wanted to debate with Mr. Weinberg. His ideas were perplexing and provocative. It seemed like this scientist was presenting him with the first drops of an elixir which could connect anything and everything back to God. This man looked out at creation and saw all of it dancing in a complex pattern that sung a song for and painted a picture of its Creator. But as Paul opened his mouth to launch another counter attack, Mr. Weinberg began to fade. The room grew dark. He could barely make out bright lights and commotion above him. Paul was not sure what was happening, but something had changed very drastically. He felt pain running through his body, and all the deep thoughts which his mind had plunged into were a world away.

....

The heart monitor alarm went off as the numbers on the screen began to plummet. Suddenly, doctors and nurses rushed in and worked busily to save the man's life. What had gone wrong? Was he having an allergic reaction to the medication? Was the combination of chemicals producing unforeseen side effects? Were his organs too damaged to sustain themselves?

A lone preacher watched as they wheeled the man away into the operating room yet again. He felt the darkness of sunset closing in and wondered if Paul would see the next sunrise.

"God...have mercy."

Chapter 8 - God is Love

Yellow pastel petals floated on gentle gusts of wind scented with roses. On either side of the well-kept path stood a row of trees in full spring bloom. A river flowed and curved underneath a cobblestone bridge up ahead and trailed off to a distant waterfall. Birds chirped in the branches overhead. Paul was barefoot and the dirt beneath him felt soft and gentle on his feet. He circled around and took in the full panorama of the area.

The sun penetrated past the rustling leaves, leaving a moving collection of light dancing about the ground. Patches of moss glowed beneath the trees. Scarlet butterflies landed on Paul's arm. He had never seen such red butterflies before. Their stark red was accented by pink lines weaving elegant patterns into their wings. They fluttered around him three times before flying off. In awe Paul wondered, *Wow, this seems too perfect...too peaceful. Like someone replaced the real world with a garden... is this heaven?*

"Kind of feels that way doesn't it." Paul spun around at the sound of Grace's voice. He felt a sudden flood of emotions, all of them more intense than the scenery. Instantly his heart quickened, his palms began sweating, and more butterflies fluttered in his stomach than in the breeze. She was wearing a scarlet dress accented by pink embroidery and ribbons. A blood red rose hung behind her right ear. Paul recognized the golden chain with the three triangular prisms around her neck. He had grown to love her innocent perfection. From her barefoot feet to her cheerful smile, the warmth of the spring afternoon radiated around her gentle mystique. Her presence saturated the birds and trees until everything echoed her energy.

Paul gulped. *Well, here goes nothing...* "Grace, it always feels like heaven when I'm with you." His voice sounded more confident than expected, but his hands quivered. A breeze sent her hair dancing about, but it was her smile that drew him in. Before he had made any conscious decision to approach, Paul was standing next to her. "Shall we stroll?" Grace nodded. As they both turned to walk their hands grazed. *Should I?*

Who is God?

Paul remembered an old conversation with a brother he no longer knew. "The trick is to know when to strike. You have to couple positive feelings with your advances. Ideally, you want to distract the girl with something pleasing. For example, someone walking by with a puppy or an old couple holding hands. This simultaneously forces her attention away from you while giving her a happy feeling. Remember, she becomes more vulnerable as her emotions peak. That's the best time to make your move. You can take her hand, or put your arm around her waist, or some other forward and flirty move that will put stars in her eyes. With a little luck and time, those stars will be the only thing she's left wearing."

Paul had successfully used his brother's technique in the past. The trouble was, he had forgotten all he had ever learned. He was already so clueless that he felt light as a feather, happy as a kid on Christmas morning, corny enough to be eaten, and was almost ready to start whispering sweet nothings in Grace's ear. It felt like a little devil was on Paul's left shoulder stamping his feet and screaming, but his protests were muted by an angel playing tranquil harp music on the other. Paul was about to reach out and touch Grace's hand without one ounce of premeditated planning or beguiling intentions! Luckily for Paul's would-be devil, all this euphoria came to a crashing halt as Grace spoke.

"So Paul, did you figure out who God is yet?" Paul stopped abruptly and retracted his hand just as they reached the bridge. His jaw clenched as the hair on the back of his neck stood upright and his hands tightened into fists. *Really? I mean REALLY? Why does she have to bring this up again!?*

"Okay....who is God?" He sighed in defeat as he leaned against the bridge wall. "A lot of people have asked me that question and I've been told that God is all kinds of things. I guess it's really not surprising. I mean, think about it. People see God as themselves. Since people imagine God as perfection, he tends to look like each person's ideal version of what they want to be. To an artist, he might be a musician or a painter, and for a thinker he might be logic or science. And, of course, here you are busily working away trying to make God look like something beautiful."

"Well I do my best," his bright-eyed companion beamed back as she sat on the wall next to him.

"I suppose it takes someone as pretty as you to

make something as draconic as God look good." Paul threw his arms out in a grandiose gesture as his voice sank a couple octaves before turning sarcastic. "God is this phenomenal cosmic power... that's just a little too busy to make life easy. Don't worry though. It's really his secretary's fault. Darn Michael's been too busy pumping asteroid belts to throw in a couple miracles and organize God's schedule. Speak of the angel, no wonder why there're so many earthquakes. He should really be more careful throwing around all those stones of fire! But ya know what, let's look past the whole problem of the evil God thing."

Grace folded her arms in impatience. "Good, otherwise I was going to ask for a successful counter to my past solution to evil, and that's not gonna go well for you."

"Actually Grace, I'm pretty sure all you gave me was an explanation of how God is not a dance-hating kill joy. The problem of evil is still ripe and ready, but like I said, I'll ignore that for now. It's your cute smile–it makes me go all soft." Paul placed his arm around her shoulder.

Grace squirmed out of Paul's grasp as she rose to her feet. "*I* think you're actually intimidated by my superior physique and quick-witted mind, but I'll let that go because *your* cute smile makes me go all soft." Grace giggled as she poked Paul and darted up the bridge.

"Hey!" Paul laughed. He sprinted ahead of her and barred her path. "None shall pass!" he threatened with a glint in his eye.

"Okay Mr. Troll, I know how I can make you move." Grace cleared her throat. "And now we will, unless someone in the audience cares to develop a counter thesis, give a lengthy analysis, and I do mean lengthy, of the character of God which will unite the normative grounding of His ethical nature with His ontological status as a Triune being. Starting at point 1, subcategory A, prime..."

Paul dropped to his knees as he clasped his hands. "NO! Please, I beg you, no!" he gasped dramatically. "Anything but that! I'll do anything to stop the most beautiful woman alive from turning into my brother."

Grace placed her hands on her hips and stared Paul down. "Well...what are you waiting for Mr. Audience?"

Paul did a face plant into his palm before rising

from his knees. "Okay, breathe...breathe... okay. In order to stop you from turning into Queen James, I'm gonna have to sound like him for a few minutes and then it will all be over. Now let's see if I can get through this without killing myself from boredom."

Paul started pacing up and down the bridge. "From what I can tell right now, it looks like God might be a very useful idea. Like believing in God helps some people do great things. It also looks like this ordering abstract might actually be out there, somewhere, but I'm not sure if I really know him. So who is God? I guess he's the blind, stoic equation that holds symmetry together, or something like that."

Grace shook her head. "That's better, but you still missed the most important point. Paul, God is love."

Paul again leaned against the cobblestone wall that ran down the side of the bridge. "Now that sounds a little cliché."

Grace took a step towards him. "It sounds a little cliché because it's so true that many have said it. God...is...love." Paul looked around at the dream-like place he was in. On the one hand, it did look like a loving being might create all this. But then again, what about a hurricane or tornado? Didn't God create all that too? But there was a better argument he could make, one that struck at the heart of the matter.

Paul straightened up as his tone turned serious. "So let me get this straight. You say that God is love, right? You would probably say that God loves us so much that he wants us to be his children. Okay, so why then would a loving God kill his own son? He stopped the blade with Abraham and Isaac, but for some reason he doesn't care about his own son enough to do the same. Was that love? Is hanging your son on a tree love?

"Paul, suppose I was a doctor, and you came to me with a hand infected with gangrene. Let's say you had gotten frost bite and waited far too long to seek treatment so now your whole forearm is changing color. As a doctor it is my job to take care of you, which in this case means amputating your forearm. Is it a good thing to cut off your arm? In itself no, of course not. The very thought is ghastly. But if you've killed a portion of yourself, then cutting off that dead portion is not evil, it's merciful. In fact, it would be wicked for me to withhold amputation under those circumstances.

"Now suppose you did something far worse than just cut off an extremity. What if you burned out your heart through years of misuse. Suppose you had ruined your health and were well on your way to the grave. Now imagine that the only way to save your body was for another to give his heart to you. Imagine that only a person with a healthy, pure heart who was willing to sacrifice himself for you could undo the damage that your sin had done. Would this savoir be so wicked?"

Paul scowled. "You're using an unfair analogy. The doctor or martyr didn't make the rules. Okay, if the doctor or anyone else sacrificed himself to save the patient that would be noble. But God is in a position where he made us and watched us sin. He could have stopped us, but instead he kills another in order to supposedly fix the first sin that he should have prevented. I just don't get it. If your God is so big, then why is his solution so small?"

"What do you think Jesus accomplished when he died on the cross?" The question was straightforward, but Paul didn't know what to say. He shrugged his shoulders and waited for her reply. "God is life. And I don't mean that as a mere analogy. God actually is existence. To separate yourself from God is to separate from life itself. When you sin, you fall out of harmony with God. You stop dancing with Him, but He's the one holding up both you and the dance floor. You stop playing His sheet music, but He's the one who keeps the notes on the page and the instrument in your hand. You try painting a different picture, but He's the one that creates the distinctions in the colors that you use. To divide yourself from God is to divide yourself from the very foundations of reality, which is why to do so is to damn yourself."

Despite the quickening of her speech and her rising intensity, Grace never lost her temper. Instead, she continued to hit Paul with point after point as she climbed her logical ladder one rung at a time. "In fact, the destruction that you wreak is so extensive that you cannot repair it. Think about it. For thousands of years people have wanted to lay aside their differences and just get along. They've desperately craved peace, but all the while only created more war. Their power has grown with new science, but their wisdom has faded with forgotten theology. As much as you'd like to return to life, you cannot do so on your own. You need something greater than yourself to save you from your worst enemy, who lives in your skin. And God showed you that.

"God died on a cross in order to demonstrate to you both how desperate your plight was, and how far God was willing to go in order to save you. You ask why did God do things this way? Well, I doubt that a finite being such as yourself is in a particularly good position to critique an infinite, all knowing one. But even given humanity's severe limitations of knowledge, one can still ask why would God not demonstrate His love any other way? Why would God choose to show that He was willing to save you in a way that did not involve Him sacrificing Himself?

"The most precious thing in the world to a dying man is the preservation of life. If he's dying of thirst he craves water above all else, if he's dying of hunger he craves food. You and everyone else are dying. And what does God do in order to reach you? He dies. He demonstrates that He is willing to forgo the one thing you most crave in order to show you how much He cares. He's willing to spill His blood for you so that you will see He is your water and your bread of life."

The wind grew stronger during Grace's explanation. The leaves rustled with vigor as nature shook them free. Dozens of red petals twirled around them as Paul became acutely aware of the symbolism underlying Grace's theology. It seemed like something deep and strange. God had apparently suffered greatly for the sake of making a point. But why? As if she could read his mind Grace continued. "God did all this to teach you the same lesson which underlies everything that God does and God is. God is a relational being. His very character, which is reflected in all of nature, is intrinsically personal. Nothing about Him is to be understood in isolation. If we're alone, it's because we're not walking with God. It took a drastic action on God's part to pierce through our rebellious nature and make us realize this, but God has done what we could not."

Grace put her hands on Paul's shoulders and motioned for him to turn. The two looked out at the tranquility before them. Swimming in the pristine river was a school of fish. Each one was a bright red sliver pushing along in rhythm with all his friends. Above them sat a robin in her cozy nest. She was nuzzling her young, which were too small to have yet grown feathers. Above them was another kaleidoscope of butterflies twirling in the wind. A chorus erupted as birds chirped and bull frogs croaked. The earth danced in unison with her children as water lapped the shoreline stones, and long strands of grass slowly swayed back and forth in the breeze. Everywhere was subtle motion and sound that formed a serene harmony not unlike what lived in the mind of Bach and Kinkade.

And on the bridge stood a young man and woman. The swirling wind seemed to push their hands together. At first they grazed each other and then their hands became one as their fingers interlocked. It was an amazing thing, really. Her fingers were far smaller than his. If he wanted to, he could have crushed them almost as easily as one of the birds. But he dare not harm the joy now filling his hand. He let the sensations soak into him like ointment into dry skin as her warmth made him conscious of emotions he had never experienced before.

He already knew she was a beautiful woman. The symmetry of her figure, the radiant color of her eyes, the way her hair shone in the sun, her rosy cheeks, and the redness of her lips altogether made him wonder if he was really looking at a person at all. Maybe he had stepped into heaven and now held the hand of an angel. For the first time in his life, the young man believed he had been given a gift from God.

Paul was starting to understand the point of relationship. Holding Grace's hand created that same energy that their connection on the dance floor had. Their bond produced something new, something that could not be reduced to a pair of machines in motion. Maybe that was why God always existed as multiple persons. Yes, that must be it! As three people, He was always in union, He was always in relationship, and He was always in love. Paul could not understand why an infinite being would sacrifice anything for a guy like himself, but it became immediately obvious why someone would sacrifice anything, even life itself, for someone like Grace.

Paul was so enthralled by the powerful joys Grace was sending through his hand that he hardly noticed the sun setting far too quickly. The leaves on the trees were rapidly aging and were now a brilliant shade of maroon. The spring afternoon had suddenly turned into a fall sunset that bathed a yellow, orange, and red world in the warm glow of a dying day. All he knew was that somewhere in the past several minutes...or maybe it had been hours...he had entered into relation with this woman, and he did not want to leave her. He wanted to become closer and live in greater union with her.

Once more he lifted his hands to touch her. His left hand moved over her lower back and began to pull her closer. His right moved up her side until coming to rest on her cheek. His body drew close enough for the two to talk in whispers. Paul's heartbeat sped up. She stared up at him in anticipation, hoping to hear what needed to be said. "You know I think I get it."

Grace smiled. "Really?"

Paul took a moment to once more run his eyes over her. "Yeah, I do. All this is an analogy, right? It's a message. It's supposed to tell us something about God. Dancing, music, painting, or I guess anything artistic, puts beauty into a physical form. The art describes how things were meant to be, how we were supposed to live in harmony with God and each other. And the science of light, logic, and matter, are there to show us how that harmony is always in the background, holding us together in a close embrace with God."

Grace nodded in approval and Paul continued, "So...what if I were to kiss you right now?" Grace cocked her head in hesitation. "What if we kissed? Is that another analogy? Are the sensations we feel when you take my hand or I graze your cheek, are those also there to show the relationship between us and God?" Grace nodded again. "Thank you for taking my hand, and thank you for letting me hold you now. But I must ask, may I come one step closer and kiss you?"

At that moment something in Paul died and was then born anew. He had never done that before. It violated orthodox player practice. The worst thing to do after having seized the initiative with a girl of unknown desires was to pause. By asking such a question you made it easy for the girl to push out of the traps you had laid. She could say that she really liked you but things were going too fast.

Now on the other hand, if one pressed his advantage he could reasonably push as far as a kiss without being overly aggressive. Even if the girl was uncomfortable, she would rarely ask the male to stop. And assuming she didn't, then a new least common physical denominator had been established in the relationship. Ordinarily, Paul would have known that somewhere a barrel chested, beer guzzling lumber jack must be weeping at his poor performance.

But what difference did any of that make now?

Paul did not want to take a hot rod for a hot ride. Nor would he mind slowing if Grace asked. It wasn't so much the kiss that mattered. What mattered was growing in union with Grace. Kissing her had become a means to that end, and nothing else. He was actually expecting her to say no. Instead, she pulled him closer until they were only inches apart. Paul's heart skipped a beat out of shock and nerves.

"What do you think would happen if you kissed me?" They were staring directly into each other's eyes. He knew he could kiss her without stopping for small talk if he wanted to. She was allowing him into her personal space without any apparent desire to reject him, but his tarry continued.

"I think we would feel like we were together. I think it would feel the same way it felt back on the dance floor, or when we were so close on the beach. Like there was one person, who just happened to have two bodies. And I know I would love to feel that way again. And I hope you do too."

A dark sensation washed over Paul. It felt like he had left his body and was watching himself from above his head. The intimate connection between himself and his body was growing weak. By this point, it was held in place by a thread. Paul tried to push the unnerving feeling that something was wrong out of his mind.

"Yes Paul, I would love to share that with you. I have always wanted to share that with you." Paul moved forward, but he could not remember if his lips ever met hers. Instead, the warm feeling he expected proved fleeting. The ambient background music of nature turned silent as the summer warmth turned cold. There was a lot of confusion and rushed debate below him, but he could not see what was going on.

Chapter 9 - God is a Sacrifice

The world was dim and quiet; everything felt cold. A series of shock waves ran through the dying man like lightning bolts through the ocean. Paul should have experienced extreme agony, but felt too detached to register what was happening to his body. He knew there was commotion below, but it seemed like it must involve someone else. He was too numb from the cold to feel pain right now.

As quickly as the past scenes had crept into his mind, a new setting formed. Like the others, Paul neither knew how he arrived here nor cared. He merely continued on as if his present predicament was exactly where he should be. But unlike all his past visions, this one, although it felt the most distant, was actually the closest to home. Paul saw a hospital bed where a bandaged patient lay. A nurse stood with her back to Paul. She was still, as if in deep contemplation. Tubes, syringes, and vials lay in neat trays next to the dying person, and a heart monitor steadily beeped in the background, but the nurse just stood there. Perhaps all that could be done had been done?

Paul approached the nurse and asked, "Will the patient live?" The figure shook her head. "Is the patient still alive?" Again, the figure shook her head. Paul searched for words to comfort her. "Well, I'm sure you did your best. My mother use to be a nurse, and I know it always hit her hard whenever she lost a patient. I remember her sometimes coming home in tears over it. My father would stay up all night trying to comfort her. She was a real sensitive sort, but I guess you have to be to enter this kind of work." A heavy silence enveloped the room. Paul continued talking just to avoid it.

"Did the patient believe in God? I know sometimes that helps the suffering and their families?" The nurse nodded. "Speaking of my mother, when she was dying the one thing that held her together was her belief in God. She was really convinced she was going to see Jesus when this was all said and done, and it gave her the strength to push ahead a lot longer than anyone expected–kept my Dad going too. If it weren't for his faith, I'm not sure where he would be right now.

Who is God?

Do you believe in God?"

Once more the figure nodded. Paul sensed
something was wrong. The room seemed too cold even
for a hospital, and its single, buzzing light seemed too
sickly yellow. He felt like he was being watched. Like
every move he made was being judged, and he had
been found wanting. "Please, will you tell me your
name." The figure slowly turned. Paul felt a sudden jolt
of both confusion and warmth, "What...Mom? Mom!"

Paul threw his hands around the older woman
with a strength that would have knocked her over if he
had not pulled her back. His tight embrace was
returned by a much softer, weaker one. "Mom! Wow,
you're here! What are you doing here? It's been so
long! Why? How? I..." He stepped back to look into the
mother's face that he had missed for so long and
gasped. In the midst of his excitement he had not seen
the lines over her lips. A series of thin black threads
crisscrossed back and forth. "Mom, are
those...stiches?" Her growing tears answered Paul.

Paul stepped back in fear and took in his
surroundings. The room they were in did not look like
a hospital at all. The walls were made of stone and one
heavy iron door provided the only way out. It had a

single thin slit in the middle. The room was small, and there were shackles on the walls. "This isn't a hospital?... Is this a prison? And what about this poor soul..." Paul reached out to pull the sheets back. He wanted to see the victim's face. He did not believe that a person should be left to die in such a cold, dank dungeon.

His hand never reached the cloth. With surprising speed, his mother's hand jutted forward and grasped Paul's wrist. He stared down at her hand. Her fingers were gnarled and boney and her flesh was ashen gray. Despite its wretched appearance, the fingers clamped down with enough force to make Paul wince. The woman glared at him with a staunch warning. Paul stepped back from the body, and she released her grasp.

Paul massaged the pain in his wrist. Something was strange. He had an odd sensation that his body was out of order. He could have sworn the walls were creeping in. The thoughts in his mind began racing and he started to piece together what was happening. "This isn't real, is it?" His mother's grimace made Paul regret those words. "No, that's not what I meant. I mean...I'm dreaming...or something like that. This place, it exists in my mind as much as it exists anywhere else, right?" The nurse bowed her head in approval. "Okay, so let me think this through...where am I? How did I get here?"

And then it happened. In the passing of a breadth a sharp pain pierced Paul's body. He collapsed to his knees as a series of visions penetrated his soul. The intense experiences all pounded his consciousness so quickly they overlapped. They began with the elegant motions of a beautiful woman. Then came intense anger, detached silence, viscous sarcasm, profound love, and dozens of other memories that coiled about his conscious mind. Each one seemed so new and pure it was as if he had never felt this way before. Raw pain gave way to pure ecstasy followed by rage and then bewilderment. Finally the intense flashes returned to raw pain, which left Paul gasping for breath on all fours. Vomit covered the floor beneath his mouth as his mother's gentle hands guided him to his knees. Paul was not sure how long the assault lasted, but the visions were piecing together.

"I remember meeting people. I remember meeting Grace several times... three times..." He noticed his mother's brow rise. Carefully, he rose to his feet. "I remember everything about her from the sound of her voice to the touch of her hand. She was perfect. And I remember meeting a lot of different people, in a lot of different places. When was the last time everything was normal?" Paul's mother stared at him intensely, hanging on every word, wanting him to continue. "So now, wait. Was it the physics teacher? He seemed like a tricky enough guy to slip me something. No, he wasn't first. James came before that. And James was doing what James always does. He kept going on and on about his new life, and as always once he started even the gates of hell couldn't get him to shut up. And that art curator. That one was half professor and half drill sergeant; she was tough, but she at least knew her stuff. And Dad. I remember Dad talking a lot about you, but then again he usually does. And then back to Grace... But no, someone came before that. Who was it?"

The fog clouding Paul's mind rapidly receded before another round of piercing images. He doubled over in agony. Only the clutching grip of his mother's hands kept him standing. Visions of old friends and past memories mingled with the present. Suddenly every gear in his mind clicked into place. What was happening to him? Why was everything finally coming into focus?

"That preacher! Yes! I remember the preacher. That crazy old puritan down by the Hell Fire Go Go Bar!" The older woman winced at the word "hell", but still loosened her grip and helped her son upright. Through heavy breathing Paul shared his thoughts aloud. "He was the last guy I talked to before somebody threw me down the rabbit hole. Yes, okay....So what does that leave me? That still doesn't tell me where I am or what I am doing." His mother stepped forward and tapped Paul's forehead. "I'm trying, mom...." She stretched out the palm of her empty left hand towards the ceiling. Then she pretended to grab something from it with her right hand. Finally, she reached forward and tapped Paul's head again.

"I'm sorry Mom, but I really don't get what you're trying to tell me. You want to what? Put something in my head? You've been trying to do that my whole life and it still hasn't worked." Paul's mother made the same motion with her hands, only this time she tapped his heart. "Okay, so you're trying to put something in my what? Emotions, soul, philosophical disposition... wait... everyone here has been trying to teach me something." She placed her hand on Paul's shoulder and nodded rigorously. "All right, so you're trying to do the same thing that everyone else has been doing. This prison cell and you are here to teach me something...and I suppose that something is about God, right?" The nodding continued.

"So what is it? ...am I supposed to learn something about suffering?" His mother's pained expression confused him. He watched her lips strain against their stitches until he placed his fingers over them. "That's not going to help, you've suffered enough.... Mom, what did they do to you?" He gave her a gentle hug, as if she were made of porcelain. "I really wish you could tell me who did this to you," he said looking into her eyes, hoping to find an answer there. "I'd love to..." Paul's hands clenched into tight fists as the muscles throughout his body tightened. A look of horror ran across his mother's face as she frantically reached out and held her son's face. The light in the room flickered for a second and returned with a slightly redder shade. Paul relaxed his grip.

"I'm sorry Mom. I'll focus harder. So, I am here to learn something. Suffering is not the answer, but whatever it is that I am supposed to learn it has to be different from all the other lessons. Everyone else taught me that God was something beautiful. God was a painter, a dancer, a musician, and a scientist...God was even love. But this doesn't match any of that. It seems like...

The thought was as obvious as it was blunt. "Mom, is this Hell?" The woman's stoic eyes and shaking head told him no. "I guess that was a stupid question. If there is one thing I am sure about it's that if there is a hell, then you're not there. But still, something is wrong. If I'm not in hell, am I dying?"

Paul's mother teared up. Nothing about this situation made sense. Every step so far had a purpose. He did not believe that God was a dancer, but at least he knew what Grace was trying to do on the dance floor, or what Mr. Weinberg was doing in the classroom, and so on. But now he felt like he was trapped in hell even though the one person here was the one person he knew would not go to hell. Was her love reaching out across time and space? Was her spirit there to guide him away from a fiery gate? Or was he even talking to his mother at all? Was all this just going on in his head? He needed answers and had no way to find them.

Oh wait! I got it!" Paul rummaged through the vials on the cart. He peered over at the body in the bed. Sorry, but I don't think you're going to need any of these now." Paul grabbed a syringe and then handed it to his muted mother.

"Can you spell it out?" Her eyes grew big as she realized what Paul was suggesting. *The bags under her eyes look so large I can't imagine when she last slept. What have they done to her? This can't be heaven. But if my mother's here I know it can't be hell. Maybe I'm just running out of time...* She eagerly grabbed the syringe and began diligently spraying its contents onto the granite wall. She worked carefully, but the letters dripped and were still difficult to read. Just as she emptied the syringe she finished her message. Scrawled onto the wall in dripping red letters was one word.

"Sacrifice"

Paul stared, dumbfounded. Sacrifice? The concept was so familiar that it felt strange. On the one hand, he had heard that Jesus was a sacrifice hundreds of times. Every sermon he had ever suffered through wailed away at this point. Christ died to pay the penalty for our sins. He bore the weight that we could not. Even Grace had made a point to say that God had sacrificed himself for us. That was how he showed his love to sinful beings that had separated themselves from him, that had doomed themselves to die by refusing to embrace life. But those words had never made sense to Paul. God was at best a distant abstract and at worst an angry judge who measured people by standards that they could not understand. Somehow those bloody letters on the wall did not seem like they could reach all the way up to heaven, and if anything, were more fit for hell.

"God suffered? God suffered for us. God suffered for his children. But why? Grace already told me the answer. God suffered in order to show his love... "For God so loved the world that he... gave His only begotten son." Paul repeated the words he heard time and again while growing up. His mother beamed. Once again tears welled in her eyes, this time from joy. She reached forward and held her son's hands with her own frail fingers. Though her eyes glowed with love, her skin was as cold as freezing iron chains.

The light flickered again. This time the pause in darkness was longer. The smile on mother's face waned. The terrible feeling that something was watching him crept into Paul's mind again. He could almost feel eye lashes on the back of his neck. He turned to look behind him, but his mother stayed his body with a gentle hand. She drew closer and looked deeply into her son's eyes. The expression reminded him of Grace. He longed to leave this place and return to her arms as much as he longed to remove his mother from this wretched hell hole.

"Mom, can we leave this place?" Her brow wrinkled, but she never nodded one way or the other. "Can you leave this place?" Again, she gave no clear answer. "What lies beyond the door?" Paul turned to examine that heavy metal slab. It was old and rusting and matched the shackles on the walls. *This isn't where they put people to get well. This is where they put them to rot and die.* "This is an asylum, isn't it? Those shackles on the walls are there to restrain patients, and the slit in the door is for observation." Paul didn't bother to turn and see his mother's slow nod. He stepped towards the door. The light flickered as he reached out for the handle. *That's strange...is the light turning more red with each flicker?* "Ah!" He jerked his hand away from the door in surprise, for the metal was so cold it was painful to touch. His mother moved to comfort him and held his wrists again, examining his hands. Her touch was soft. She clearly wanted him to stay, but also did not have the strength to keep him there. Paul's attention was drawn back to the bed.

"Who lies under that blanket? Who died in this cruel place?" Paul's mother only shook her head no, but Paul needed answers. He slowly approached the corpse on the table. Each step reverberated against the cold stone around him. Again he reached forward to pull back the bed sheet. A woman's scream rang out and stayed his hand a second time. The painful sound shot through his body as it bounced off the walls and echoed in his head. There was a loud bang and the sharp scraping of iron and metal. Paul doubled over and grabbed at his head to shut out the sound. It was over in an instant and Paul spun around to find an empty room and an open door. "No! MOM!" In desperation, he darted out of the room leaving the single light and corpse behind.

The hallway outside of the cell was barren. In either direction rows upon rows of great doors stood next to each other in close succession. A sickly yellow light illuminated the corridor in front of each one. The number 1 3 was roughly carved into the door. *Can't forget that number.* He chanted them to himself as he rushed out into the hall. Neither the right nor the left looked any different, so when his first step brought him closer to the right Paul followed his instinct. As he ran blindly down the hall he realized his feet were wet. There were dark sticky puddles on the ground, but Paul did not stop to look. He needed to find his mother.

He pushed forward for some time. As his lungs began burning for air a second blood-curdling scream rang out forcing him to cover his ears. Pain seared through his head. As much as he wanted it to stop, he knew he needed to follow the horrid sound and find his mother. But the noise seemed to be coming from both ends of the hall at the same time. Frantically, he looked back and forth. The hall was empty. The screaming continued as the pain surrounded him and threatened to engulf his senses. It was as if the very stones his feet pounded were slowly bleeding agony. As he doubled over yet again, he caught a glimpse of a nearby puddle that he had just run through...its dark red color betrayed its darker contents.

Who is God?

Paul woke up on the floor. A sickly yellow light was buzzing above him and jolted him back to his current reality. He bolted up and vomited again when he saw all the blood covering his cloths. The hall was silent. He had no idea how long he'd been out or where his mother might be. A dreadful thought ran through Paul's head. The idea might just get him exactly what he was looking for, an answer. Yet, he was no longer sure he could handle one. *I can't....I can't...but I have no other choice...* Trembling, Paul approached the nearest door. He planned on working up the nerve to push it open despite his quivering arms, but as he leaned against it, the door effortlessly swung open on its own. Paul peered into the room in awe.

It was well lit and filled with color. Confused, he entered and was overwhelmed by the sweet aroma of hundreds of flowers. *What the...* Paul thought as he walked around the exotic plants and flowering shrubs. Every petal was a brilliant shade of royal red, crimson, or scarlet. Thick, green forest vines grew up the walls. The entire room was alive and growing. Only the eerie silence reminded him of the dungeon he had just stepped out of. Paul's hallow pacing and heavy breathing seemed magnified in the void.

Paul walked up and down the room's aisles. He admired each plant until he came to a very familiar one. The rose bush was as red as any blood he had ever seen. The color was so vibrant it looked as if the flower had grown a heart of its own. Paul reached out to touch the petals, expecting to feel soft fibers reminiscent of Grace's softer skin. To his surprise, the petals felt cold and the rose crumbled, fragmenting into dust. Paul watched, frozen with fear as the decay traveled down the length of the flower and spread rapidly to the whole bush. Within minutes death had spread to every plant in the room. Paul looked back to where the rose had stood, but it was gone. Only a pile of ash and thorns remained. The petals were also gone; in their place lay Paul's outstretched hand covered in blood. Paul pulled back from the death before him and fled from the haunted garden out into the hall again. The door effortlessly shut behind on its own accord. Disoriented and longing for some place safe and familiar, Paul traveled hesitantly down the hallway back in what he thought was the direction of cell number 13.

He had traveled down about 7 cells when he came to one with muffled noise emanating from behind

the heavy iron door. It sounded like...voices. He placed
his ear against the door eager to hear a friendly voice,
but the words were still too muffled to understand.
*Okay, now what...maybe it's someone who knows a
way out of this place...then again what if it's Mom... or
her tormentors? Okay, I can do this. This is just a
nightmare, I'll wake up soon. Just keep looking for a
way out.* His hand trembled as he reached forward and
pulled back the slit in the iron door. He moved to
observe the "patient", if any such unfortunate soul
lived behind that barrier. *Okay, I can do this, here we
go.* He took a deep breath and slowly peered in. The
large, crowded courtroom with rich, mahogany walls
was the last thing Paul expected to see.

The room was filled with hundreds of creatures.
There were lions, oxen, eagles, and many others.
Sitting to the side were a dozen human looking jurors
dressed in white robes. They were all fixated on one
slick, archetypal lawyer. He had the sharp, strong
features of an attractive man combined with the
smooth, silky voice that could make a woman's heart
melt. His black suit and tie, white button down shirt,
and groomed hair looked too perfect to be human. The
man paced back and forth across the courtroom with

so much intuitive elegance that it looked as if he had been made for this. Before the man had finished his first sentence, Paul already knew he wanted to agree with him, regardless of what the lawyer had to say.

His smooth voice began gently. "We all trust the law. We are all expected to live by the law, and if need be, we are expected to be punished by the law. The law is the great equalizer. It is what structures our interactions with one another. Without it, this world would descend into chaos and promises made in covenant would be worthless. Without it, covenant promise would be worthless, and all would be fair. Thus, the law must be applied, and it must be applied universally. To make exception to the law is to make our organizing principle arbitrary. To do so would both compromise the integrity of the law, and he who makes the law."

The lawyer glanced up at the judge as murmurs traveled through the audience. Paul sensed that this last statement caught them off guard, that they were not expecting such a bold declaration. He wanted to see the judge's face, but the presiding presence was just out of his field of view. The lawyer seemed quite aware of the provocative stance he had just taken. He absorbed the frightened murmurs with a satisfied smile and waited just long enough for his words to settle before continuing with more intensity.

"The defendant is guilty of violating the law. That much has been proven beyond a shadow of a doubt. His list of crimes is numerous despite his youth. In a small number of years, the defendant has managed to, at least in spirit, break every single commandment we have. He has lied and lusted, gluttonized and gossiped, and become so enraged with hatred that only mere temporal and physical limitations restrained the violent desires underlying his anger. This man has blamed others for his blasphemy and mocked anyone willing to extend a hand. But the most disturbing thing about this particular man, and regrettably this is indicative of his entire era, is his slothful lack of ambition."

The lawyer's eyes grew wide. He looked like he would taste the words if he could, as if he wanted to leave the courtroom to be left alone with that one statement as it slid across his tongue and resonated in his ears. "This man had talent and resources in droves. A keen intellect, well, keen by the relevant human standards..." The lawyer's smile was dripping with delighted sarcasm.

Paul felt an uneasiness creep into him the longer he listened. He had never seen a lawyer take such satisfaction in another's plight. Paul had joked with his brother that only lobbyists rivaled lawyers' sophistry. He often said it is no wonder that these straight laced pretty boys typically endured many attacks against their character, for they so often championed the highest bidder. But even if one were to buy all the bad lawyer jokes in the world, something about this one transcended truth for hire. No, this man was enjoying his attacks against the defendant. He seemed invigorated by the thought of crushing a man's soul.

Now the lawyer's voice sounded emboldened by his pleasure, and continued with new volume and accompanying motion. "He could have created a powerful synergy with that intellect and charisma. Some have one or the other, but few have both. But like so much dust before him, he was content to let his dominion fade back into the earth. It appears he was not worthy of that which was bestowed upon him." Again, murmurs went up from the court room. This time they were louder and more frustrated. Only a single loud crack from what must have been a gigantic gavel silenced the protestors. The lawyer seemed pleased by the dissent he was brewing, and his voice grew in volume yet again as excitement over his words continued.

"Oh, do I offend you? Forgive me, but I cannot help but notice how much these mammals, these animals, act out their inherent limitations. I'm afraid I lack the...limitless patience of the infinite." Again the crowd murmured, and again the gavel cracked. This time the lawyer glared at the judge as he smiled.

"So in the interest of the law the man must receive the fullest penalty which is worthy of his crime. We all know the depth of the punishment which hath been declared for similar past transgressions." A cruel grin crossed the man's lips as they poured forth sarcasm. Paul's stomach churned. "Now, in the interest of fairness, in the interest of not compromising the noble character of the even more noble law giver, I humbly ask for consistency in the application of the law." And with that the lawyer turned his head, stared directly into Paul's soul, and spat his next words with a husky, guttural tone unfitting for his fair features. "Kill him!" Paul gasped as he stepped back from the door and turned to run. He only made it a couple steps before the lights died, leaving nothing but darkness and silence.

Paul's breathing was heavy as his heart pounded in his ears. *What is happening! How much worse can this get! This whole place is death and I'm trapped here. Gotta find a way out!* Paul tried to move as quickly as he could, but had to go slow in the dark. Each step was premeditated. Without his vision, all his other senses became critical. He had to be able to hear someone coming. He tried to calm his heart and control his heavy breathing without success; it was as if his body was getting away from him. Moments dragged into hours. Despite the cold, Paul's shirt was drenched in sweat that mingled with blood. And then a light up ahead began to flicker.

The erratic bulb was fitting: A dying red light for a dying world. When the light flickered on, Paul could see markings on the walls ahead. They were haphazard and ran in every direction. They were all blood red, and all dripping so badly they barely resembled English. Still, Paul could find one or two barely legible words. They all spelled the same thing.

"Sacrifice."

The flickering light hung next to a slightly ajar door. On it lay a series of scratched out numbers that once read 1-3 but were now covered by dripping red digits that read, "666."

For a moment he stood surrounded by darkness and the many unseen sacrifices. *This is INSANE! I'm being led about like a dog on a leash. Someone is toying with me, trying to break me down. I'm stuck like a rat running through a changing maze. The only thing I know for certain is that I shouldn't be here, my Mother is in pain, and that lawyer wants me dead!*

Paul moved to push the heavy iron door. It slowly screeched open. The room looked exactly as he had left it except for the addition of the many scribbled "sacrifices" on the walls. Paul stood in the dark hall for some time, afraid to stay where he was but also too terrified to step into the light. Without knowing what else to do, Paul forced himself onward. As soon as he cleared the door's path, the heavy iron swung back with a sudden force that rattled the trays. Paul spun around and clutched his chest. He leaned against the wall for support. The flickering red light had grown so dim he could barely see two yards in front of him.

Paul's gaze returned to the bed. He felt

compelled to remove the sheet. He was certain he did not want to see the dead person under it. He was certain that looking at a corpse would be nauseating, but felt he had been led back here for a reason, and was compelled to move onward. His hand trembled more than when he had pulled back the observation slit in the lawyer's door, but Paul knew what he had to do. *Your light is fading. If you want to know what is under that blanket here is your only chance. Do it.* In one fluid motion Paul pulled the sheet with such force that he nearly tore it off the bed.

With a crushing blow he realized he knew the figure before him. He wished he did not have to see her like this.

"Grace."

She was beautiful as always, even in the white gown of a patient. Her skin was fair, her frame slender, and even in this light her hair still shined. But her chest did not rise and fall with the motions of breathing. Far more disturbing to see were those same stitches that covered her lips. Paul took her petite hands. They were the coldest thing he had yet touched here. He was not conscious of the great tears which welled up in his eyes and fell onto the bed beneath him, nor the great heaving sobs which shook him like a ship in a storm. All he could do was remember the wonderful sea of emotions which had flooded his heart every time he had seen his maiden, and the expanding void that pushed against his innards like a growing tumor.

If Paul had been conscious of these things, then perhaps he also would have noticed that the door behind him had opened without a sound. Perhaps he would have noticed that several pairs of beady red eyes now stared at him intently, that he was not alone. Maybe he would have turned to see them before the dying light flickered for the last time, and the many pairs of hands bore down on him like an angry mob that had been building in rage. His struggling and screaming were no use. There were too many of them, and they were all scratching, clawing, and biting. They tore his garments and in between their animalistic growls chattered back and forth. Paul would have given anything to make them stop, but the beady eyes ignored his pleading and kept making good on their master's commands.

....

The doctors and nurses all stood around Paul as they desperately worked. They had been fighting a losing battle for over an hour and by this point in time the patient looked more dead than alive. For a while things had seemed hopeful, but then taken a turn for the worse. His heart had given out and the team shocked him back to life. They held his body down as great waves of electricity ran through him, but all the convulsing did was make things look more hopeless. All the while, a preacher nervously paced outside in the waiting room, embroiled in a frantic internal monologue with God.

All right God, you brought this young man into my life for a reason. You do everything for a reason. I have been preaching to a lifeless body for many hours now, but then again we are all dead men without Christ and all preaching is initially done to corpses. I don't know if he heard anything I said. But I do know that he, like everyone else, can hear your Word. I know that no power, neither distance nor time, can restrain your Word if you choose to speak. So speak God, speak into this boy's heart and let him know you before it's too late.

Chapter 10 – God is Life

Paul hated the ragged face staring back at him. Blood ran down its forehead and neck, and its sweat-drenched, matted hair wavered in the howling wind as its body quivered with animalistic rage. It desperately pleaded, "No...Why?" The words echoed in the empty world in which they stood. Only the crows sitting on the dead branches above them answered back as their squawking taunted Paul from their spindly perch. Paul stood before the face with a clenched jaw and tightened fists, ready for a fight. He knew this creature was completely mad. Even though the reflection was trapped within an obsidian stone black enough to swallow the night, the darkness could not tamper the burning in its bloodshot eyes. Paul knew this face. He had seen it before. The reflection was his own.

The stone's unhewn edges were harsh and jagged. Carved deep into the rock's surface, as if to make sure no one would ever forget them, were cruel words that cut deep into Paul.

"Here lies Grace."

Paul's cheeks were red with heat and his eyes filled with watery sorrow. No one was around to see this. No one was here to hold his growing rage in check or appreciate his pain; no one but the crows and God. He glared up at the sky. *Come on you coward. Show me your face.* Paul paced back and forth, overflowing with contempt. He started speaking in little more than a whisper more ragged than the stone. It did not matter. His audience could hear thoughts, let alone quiet words.

"So...this is it? This is your sacrifice? Of all the people in the world, dear God, YOU had to pick this one?" growled Paul as he pointed towards the growing storm clouds in the distance. "Why?! Huh?! What does it prove? That you have all the power and hold all the cards? As if you weren't the invincible, almighty Alpha and Omega! No one has ever truly challenged you and no one ever will. You could speak us out of existence, cast us into hell, or silence our lips with stitches and death at any time you wanted. Well, forgive this poor mortal soul if you can find it somewhere deep within your black chasm of a heart, but I dissent."

Paul's volume rose as he ran his fingers over the lifeless, black stone. "She loved you, did ya know that? Did you know that she was always the first to sing praises to your so called holy name? She wanted nothing more than to describe you in the most beautiful of terms. You were a dancer, you were light, and you..." Paul's body was shaking. He slammed his fist into the nearby tree. The force of the blow sent the crows fleeing. He spat his words in frustration: "You pitiful intolerable ghost, ever absent in need but always present in judgment, YOU WERE LOVE! Did you know that?"

Paul's speech oscillated between guttural and loud with sweeping physical gestures accompanying every sentence. "Of course you did." He spewed sarcastically. "Because you know everything. There isn't a sparrow in the field that you don't know. There's not a hair on her head that you didn't count. I think it's sooo wonderful that somewhere out there in never-land there's a mind who knows all this stuff. But then, you must have known when you made her where she would end up and how she would get there. You must have known that man in his frail nature could not jump through the hoops you built or pass the tests you wrote. You knew we were going to fail, so why are we even here? Why did you tell us to look but never touch, or taste but never swallow?"

Paul worked himself into such a rage that he shouted every word. He was vaguely aware that the storm clouds were drawing nearer as the wind grew into a swirling vortex above him. "So why? What was the point? Relation? Was that it? You wanted to be in relation with us? Well, again please forgive this finite, fallible mind, but how do you have a relationship with a corpse?! Why not put a statue in the garden? Stone never would have disobeyed, and even stone is more alive than the death you put us through. No, we were not made for a relationship with you. So why?"

Unknowingly, Paul had made his way over to a brown scar that ran through the earth. It was a dried up river bed covered by bones of what used to be beautiful red schools of fish. The sight of it made Paul's stomach churn as his hatred grew even more. "Maybe you wanted a whole stinking universe that way you could build legions of fearful victims, each one subject to your whims. Was that it? Was man made to live in fear? Is he here because you needed someone smaller than yourself to pick on? Was being God not enough, so you had to be slave master too? Does the sound of innocent screams fill that absent face of yours with a smile? Does the smell of sulfur imbue your soul with a warm glow? As if an infinite being needed to be reminded of his power."

Paul followed the length of the bank in the direction of the bridge he had stood on with Grace, remembering the warmth of her hand and his desire to kiss her. There was nothing left but a pile of rubble. "Well you're not my master. You hear that? I don't serve a God that let's these things happen. I don't see what's so impressive about a God that takes something as beautiful and pristine as Grace and sacrifices her just to satisfy the whims of a sadistic accuser. For all I know, you might be him. Yeah, that's right. I think you're the accuser. Maybe when I saw that lawyer standing in court calling down judgment I was really looking at the lawmaker. Well, how about it? Was that you Jesus? Was that you accusing us for your own sick entertainment in a cosmic house of horrors? I bet only a mind as totally depraved as your own could ever dream of something so demonic?!"

Great gusts of wind blew from every direction sending frozen rain pelting towards the earth. The darkness was only broken by distant arcs of lightning. The rain's dull pain and the thunder's ominous growl invigorated Paul. A fire was burning deep within him that poured out through his maddened, bloodshot eyes and the wicked smile that creased his satisfied face. He was defying God. He, mere skin and bone, was shaking his fist towards the heavens and despite the Creator's awesome power, the God of this universe would not make one measly flesh bag bow the knee and worship. The great king loudly proclaimed his pronouncements from his seat in heaven, and Paul stood ridged before the wrathful onslaught like the righteous rebel.

"Okay God, here I am. It's you and me. You can kill me the same way you have killed so many before. You can take my life or splatter me against your hard earth until all that remains is the same dust you began with. But if you're the tree of life and in order to continue on I need to know you, to grow closer to that maniacal madman in the sky, than I choose death! You hear me? I choose death. Some say better to rule in hell than serve in heaven. Well I go further. I say, better to DIE in hell than serve in heaven!"

A lightning bolt pierced the night sky and

thundered so close it was almost on top of him. The deafening sound forced the rebel's hands to his ears as pain shot through his head, but Paul recovered his audacity. "Is that the best you can do God! Huh?!" He challenged.

God finally spoke back.

Hundreds of bolts showered the earth as if they wanted to outnumber the rain drops. Bolt after bolt crashed into the ground, shattered trees into explosions of burnt bark, and left scorched ground dotting the landscape.

Paul saw the wind circle over Grace's tombstone until it grew into a great vortex. His feet dug into the dirt as every muscle in his body pushed against the invisible, howling force moving against him. Suddenly he lost his footing. The wind dragged him away from the bridge and along the ground like a rag doll towards the cyclone over the tombstone. Paul twisted and tumbled over himself before he barely planted his feet. Shaking, he wiped the blood from his lips as he muttered, "I'm not giving up that easy." But even in the midst of this defiance, Paul knew he needed to find something to latch onto to resist the wind. He frantically scanned the horizon for something to lay hold of.

"Why does everything have to be so dead?" Paul had been pulled too far from the bridge to reach what was left of its stone walls. The only solid thing left to grab within reach was another lone, spindly tree. He exerted all his strength in an effort to inch his way towards this pillar. He stretched out his arm. As his fingers closed around the nearest branch, lightning struck the aging wood. The force ripped bark into thousands of tiny pieces and flung Paul back. Splintering shards dug into his flesh as his salvation was reduced to ash. The wind dragged him along as he tumbled about. Finally, Paul's sliding came to a crashing halt as he slammed into a rocky outcrop. Terrified, he latched onto the stones now stained with his blood.

Paul's skin burned from the heat of the blast and his muscles tore from exertion. He sat up trembling as the realization of what he'd done swirled around him and his resolve began to slip. *Why am I...even trying...God is too strong...too powerful...I...I...* Rationally, Paul was right. His resistance made no sense. How could anyone run from God? After all, Paul could not even find refuge within the confines of his own mind, for he was a sinner in the hands of a very, very angry God.

Paul rose to his feet in one last desperate stand. His body heaved under exhaustion as he shouted back at God. "NO! THIS IS NOT OVER! I AM NOT GIVING IN!"

But God was not to be outdone.

Jagged pain shot through his legs. Paul screamed as its force brought the man to his knees. He toppled over and clutched his legs. "ALRIGHT! You're angry! I'm sorry. I just don't understand! Everyone says you're love, but why did Grace have to die? What does it prove if..." Paul never finished his sentence. His lips pressed together against his will as he felt the treads of the stitches form.

Paul panicked as his life began to fade away. *No... Not now! This can't be happening! I have to live! GOD PLEASE NO!* Another wave of searing agony sent his body into convulsions. His lips pulled at the stitches so hard that they tore through and he bellowed a scream that pierced the night with a volume to rival the thunder.

"I'M SORRY! PLEASE, I'M SORRY! JUST DON'T KILL ME! I DON'T WANT TO DIE! I WANT TO LIVE

GOD! I JUST WANT TO LIVE!"

All the strong words and taunting had been replaced by fear as the young man's audacity shattered like the trees before the tempest. He stood on the brink of utter annihilation. He knew the infinite could tear his soul asunder. He had even asked God to do it. And God would not be mocked.

Paul saw the eye of the storm before him. All the swirling rains and wind were spinning around one central fulcrum where the tombstone had stood. In its place, a great bush, several times the size of the stone it discarded, towered over Paul. But it was not the bush itself that paralyzed Paul with terror. No, it was the great storm of fire, the holy conflagration that consumed the bush without burning it and all the forces of nature that dragged him towards the thorned giant.

The fire was growing in power and intensity. God's wrath was seething. His anger and jealously had taken a physical form that filled the world with the same energy that flowed through nature and gave the breath of life. The heat overpowered Paul's senses. His legs would not carry him and his feeble attempts to crawl away were dwarfed by the growing font of fury pulling him in. Paul knew if he did not escape, God would burn the flesh from his bones and melt the rest. He cried out with the last breath his taxed lungs could muster in the suffocating heat.

"FORGIVE ME GOD!

The fire rose in a great pillar that stretched into the sky. It climbed and pulsed until the red tower soared as high as the eye could see and circled about like a great, consuming tornado. A trembling coursed through the ground. Shock waves rattled Paul's bones and splintered the earth beneath him. Finally, a great heave from the pillar sent the fire pushing out in all directions.

Fire washed over Paul like a tsunami over a shell at the water's edge. The heat scorched every nerve in his body, knocking and tumbling him about. When the fire receded a moment later, Paul remained somehow preserved like the bush. His clothes had been burned off, steam rose from his scarred skin, and blood poured from open wounds. The crippled man lay strewn about on his stomach, naked and exposed. Paul trembled with pain, but even in the agony which he now felt, a new growing terror sucked the breath from his lungs. What if this being, this Lord of Lords and King of Kings, decided to speak? Surely God had done enough to him?

And then the Lord answered Paul's thoughts out of the whirlwind, and bellowed with a deep voice,

> "Who is this that darkeneth counsel by words without knowledge? Gird up now thy loins like a man; for I will demand of thee, and answer thou me. Where wast thou when I laid the foundations of the earth? Declare, if thou hast understanding. Or who shut up the sea with doors? And said, Hitherto shalt thou come, but no further: and here shall thy proud waves be stayed? Hast thou commanded the morning since thy days; and caused the dayspring to know his place; Hast thou entered into the springs of the sea? Or hast thou walked in the search of the depth? Have the gates of death been opened unto thee? Or hast thou seen the doors of the shadow of death? Hast thou perceived the breadth of the earth? Declare if thou knowest it all. Where is the way where light dwelleth? And as for darkness, where is the place thereof, and that thou shouldest know the paths to the house thereof? Knowest thou it, because thou wast then born? Or because the number of thy days is great? Hast thou entered into the treasures of the snow? Or hast thou seen the treasures of the hail, which I have reserved against the time of trouble, against the day of battle and war? By what way is the light parted, which scattereth the east wind upon the earth? Who hath divided a watercourse for the overflowing of waters, or a way for the lightning

of thunder; to cause it to rain on the earth,
where no man is? Or on the wilderness, wherein
there is no man? To satisfy the desolate and
waste ground; and to cause the bud of the
tender herb to spring forth? Hath the rain a
father? Or who hath begotten the drops of dew?
Out of whose womb came the ice? And the hoary
frost of heaven, who hath gendered it? The
waters are hid as with a stone, and the face of
the deep is frozen."

The voice of God echoed across the landscape. As
the words died the fire retreated and the world
plunged into bitter frost. The scolding fire had
scorched Paul's skin, and the cold ravaged what was
left. Paul's dripping sweat froze as he lay cold and
naked, sprawled across the darkening tundra. He did
not want to move or think. All Paul wanted to do was
die. He hoped this would end his suffering. He thought
that surely now death would come and halt this pain.
But it was not to be.

The scenery shifted. He was surrounded by the
murky waters and muddy patches of swamp land. A
soft, eerie blue light emanated from everywhere. And
something was moving. Shambling past him were
dozens, maybe hundreds, of gaunt figures. Their skin
tightly clung to their skeleton frames, their cloths were

mere rags, and none wore shoes. Slowly they marched unceasingly past him with vacant expressions.

Paul stared in bewilderment. *What the...?* *They're so...lifeless. They look more dead than... NO!* Paul stared down at his hands. The skin was marred and warped. The fire and ice had left it looking like leather, just like the living dead around him. *Is that what's happening to me? I'm turning into one of them!* Paul shifted his weight in a forced effort to stand. His broken body heaved against its own mass while he gritted his teeth. Every motion felt unnatural. He had to concentrate just to open and close his hands. Paul cast his gaze towards heaven.

Why don't you just KILL ME?!

Forcing himself to his knees, Paul saw an empty beer can out of the corner of his eye. The mundane object looked out of place in this surreal environment. Bewildered, he scanned the horizon and saw other items haphazardly strewn about. There was a television set to his left, and a couple comic books to his right. A speaker, leather jacket, chrome car rims, a silver ring, and various other odd objects were buried across the hazy, blue fog.

Is this hell? It must be! Maybe there's a way out.

Maybe God's gonna give me another chance.

Yeah...maybe I can still find a way out of this place.

Just one more chance...

"I am afraid that is very unlikely." Paul turned towards the monotone, guttural voice and saw the back of a gaunt figure. It wore the same ragged clothes as everyone else, as well as a great hood which covered its head. "Your body is wasting away, your time to speak has passed". Paul brought his hand to his lips and felt a thin filament locking his jaw in place. "You have already been given far more than most. Both family and stranger alike pleaded with you. Your mother's spirit in particular traveled a great distance to find you, and I fear even her pious good sense may have failed to open your eyes. Now you must come."

The figure proceeded forward. Paul wanted to cry out with a hundred questions but the stitches forced his silence. All he could do was shamble after the phantom.

"You want to know where we are and who these people are. That is, after all, what you were thinking." Paul now felt even more naked. "Before you lays the ramifications of your life. You can see both cause and effect... I sense that you do not understand. That is regrettable but not surprising. In life you chose to live for the moment. The entirety of your being was directed towards wine, woman, and song, for tomorrow you would die. And so you did. And now you can see how you lived.

"Observe every few paces another worthless item. Go ahead, try to touch one of them. Go on. Yes, that's it, try to pick up that leather jacket. Notice how your hand passes right through it? All that you collected during your lifetime is comparable and has faded into memory. You cannot ride your bike or drive your car or wear your old cloths...including your brother's 'So Many Girls, So Little Time' t-shirt to your left. Now all that you have is...well, yourself... Oh really? Come now, is that the best you can do? Even now your thoughts immediately turn to your own losses. I suppose this is once again, to be expected.

"Let me direct your attention to the other noteworthy aspect of your surroundings, namely the people. I'll give you a hint. You could have provided at least three, maybe four, starving children with enough food, medicine, and education for a year with the money it cost to buy... how about that pile of joints over there? Their absence could have saved the little boy walking next to them.

"What? What is this that I sense in your mind? Protest? Oh, yes of course. These people lived far away so you could not have owed them anything. You never even met most of them! Some of them would not be born for many years after your own death. Yes, yes, their suffering could not possibly be credited to you. That is, of course, assuming that the meaning of your life was to, oh how do those dreadful expressions go... 'do your own thing', or 'live for the moment', or 'be true to yourself'. How about your generation's creed of 'drugs, sex, and rock and roll'? Yes, if you would have helped these people you would not have been chasing after what you wanted to do, which of course was the pursuit of your own idol entertainment executed in the grandest way possible.

"But who gave you the right to do this with your life? Was it you? Of course not! You did absolutely nothing to deserve existence. That was a gift. Did you earn such a right? What could you have possibly done to deserve letting others die so you could live in idol pleasure? No, you did nothing and have nothing by which you can alleviate your responsibility to your fellow man. You, whether you like it or not, have always had the responsibility to love thy neighbor as thyself."

The sheer number of bodies meandering by put a slimy feeling deep in Paul's gut. Was he really responsible for all these people? There must have been hundreds moving through the rolling fog, and who knows how many more were out of sight.

"I can sense your growing discontent. You think I suggest that you were required to give every spare coin away. That may be admirable, but it is not the only way to give God your first fruits. You could have utilized your talents and become a productive member of society. You also could have spent time developing relationships with people who needed them. And you could have shown proper submission to your parents, or pursued one of a hundred other noble deeds. Giving to God is not always a matter of money, in fact most of the time it isn't. No, giving to God is a matter of using the abilities and resources you were granted in order to love thy neighbor. But instead you ignored your responsibility. Every once in a while you might have done something nice in order to bask in your own self-righteousness, but by in large you allowed most opportunities to do good to pass by, and even when you made use of them the final product was still rags made filthy by selfish ambition.

"So now you are dead. And we are going someplace you will not like. Unfortunately you have no choice but to go there. You can run no longer. Now you must see the full ramifications of what you have done. Paul, look behind you."

Paul did not want to turn. He had seen so many horrid things, and felt so much pain, that he was certain whatever lurked behind him would only cause more grief. But as the shrouded figure said, there was no choice. Slowly the naked and silenced man shivering in his own frozen, bloody sweat turned to see what he had done.

And there the man hung. He was naked and beaten like Paul. Nailed to a cross, covered in lacerations, and wearing a crown unfit for criminals. "You see Paul, by embracing sin you did more than just violate a list of dos and don'ts. You embraced death. Every figure passing by you now suffered needlessly. You had the power to help them in any number of ways, but not the desire. You valued your own status symbols, your fancy cloths, and fast paced playboy lifestyle. That meant more to you than they did. And that's why you love death more than life, and why you have received the true object of your desires.

By contrast, that man on the cross did something radical. He did something that even the lawyer back in the courtroom never imagined would work. He physically lived as you did. He lived as a man, with all the frailties and weaknesses inherent to your sinful flesh. And He chose to never forget the people walking by us. He chose to go to that cross before He needlessly plucked but one useless object from this ground. He did what you chose not to; He loved his neighbor as Himself.

So why should He save you now? Since you did not love your neighbor as yourself it is obvious that you did not love Him. Why should God show love to those who do not love Him? Why would He not give you exactly what you wanted?" Even if Paul could have spoken, there was nothing left to say. He had chosen a life that fell infinitely short of that which the figure on the cross had chosen, and now there was no excuse. If he had all the powers of persuasion that the accuser possessed, Paul knew it would still be futile to utter a single word. He had chosen death, and now he would have it.

Who is God?

Paul turned to face the shrouded figure behind him. It was facing him now from only an arm's length away. It lowered its hood for the first time and revealed its face. The skin was stretched and decaying, just as all the other victims. The few visible strands of hair were brittle and grayed. But the eyes looked familiar, and Paul burst forward. *"Grace?"* He reached out to touch her face. She was ugly now. There was no denying it. Her worn skin had turned coarse and was cold to the touch, but Paul did not care. He clasped both his hands around her and pressed his sewn shut lips against hers. Paul felt the warmth of another against his own decaying skin. He felt her lips press against his own and what was left of her hands clutch his back. He was not sure if that warmth was meant to share acceptance or show him a glimpse of what was meant to be, but he kissed her all the same and for a fleeting moment felt alive again. Then their bodies withered and broke just as the red rose had done. Fractures appeared across the entirety of their frames as their bodies dissolved into dark powder. But before both people crumbled into a single pillar of ash Paul kissed Grace deeply and held her close one last time. Of all their flesh, bone, and clothing nothing remained but three triangular crystal prisms with no chain to hold them together.

Chapter 11 – God IS

Mo watched Paul's chest slowly rise and fall. It was only a matter of time now. The operating room had been a catastrophe and after being starved of oxygen too long, there was little left of Paul's mind. He had already died on the operating table and been brought back from the brink, but there was no hope of saving him again. The doctors assured Moses that they had done everything they could, but now there was nothing left to do but make the body as comfortable as possible and let nature run its course. His family would be arriving in the morning, but the doctors were confident Paul would not last until then.

Mo felt drenched in futility. This whole exercise seemed worthless. He had barely slept for the past two days and talked so much that his voice sounded raspy. And for what? So that the mind he was preaching too could burn out before it ever had the chance to respond to anything the faithful preacher had said. Mo felt like he might as well have walked into a graveyard and been preaching to the tombstones. Still, every time he looked at the poor boy sympathy would move him to press on, just in case his words were somehow reaching Paul, wherever he might be.

Mo opened his Bible to the most familiar passage in the entire book. He had both heard and preached many sermons on this one tiny chapter and now in exhaustion decided to return to it.

> The LORD is my shepherd; I shall not want. He maketh me to lie down in green pastures: he leadeth me beside the still waters. He restoreth my soul: he leadeth me in the paths of righteousness for his name's sake. Yea, though I walk through the valley of the shadow of death, I will fear no evil: for thou art with me; thy rod and thy staff they comfort me. Thou preparest a table before me in the presence of mine enemies: thou anointest my head with oil; my cup runneth over. Surely goodness and mercy shall follow me all the days of my life: and I will dwell in the house of the LORD forever.

Mo's speech was slow and methodical as his eyes trailed off and his mind wandered. "That was my wife's favorite passage. I remember how she used to find the most ridiculous times to say it. If she had done something that was bound to get me mad, like throw all my tools off the rec room table if I forgot to clean them up after a project, or hide the key to my gun case if it had been too long since I last read my Bible, I'd get all bent out of shape and try to look mad at her. Not an easy feat mind you, but I would try. And then she would look at me and quote Psalm 23. You just can't stay mad at someone quoting that Psalm. So long story short, I'd usually wind up venting my frustrations by tickling her or something equally cute. It's a good thing you didn't hear that because that probably all sounds utterly pathetic. But yeah, there was a point to what I was saying…

"Oh yes, so that was my wife's favorite passage. Now that I think about it, I don't know why I didn't read that one over and over again. You probably could use that right about now. You know this seems like a simple set of text, but I actually remember the boys going at it pretty hard back in seminary over what to do with these verses. You see, they run into this quirky little problem with the word 'return.' Depending on how you parse it, the word could be יָשֻׁב or שׁוּב. The Masoretic Hebrew and the Greek Septuagint disagree here. What that basically means is that you get a different reading if you follow the Jewish scribes from the middle ages or the more ancient Greek translation of the Old Testament. The last sentence can be justly translated: 'I will dwell in the house of the Lord', or 'I will return to the house of the Lord.'

"That leads us to two different interpretations. On the one hand, the text could be telling us that we are going to have constant access to God's temple. And sure enough, that is the exact description we get of the New Jerusalem after it descends from the sky in Saint John's Revelation. But on the other hand, it makes sense to say that we will literally dwell with God, because the Holy Ghost now lives in us. So what does it mean?

"Well, for whatever its worth I say when God puts a double meaning in the text like this there is a good chance He meant for us to see the words from a couple different angles. Yes, it is true that we will live with God in the house of the Lord, because when God dwells with us we could not do otherwise, nor would we want to. But we will also be able to continuously return to the house of the Lord after the New Jerusalem is here and God once more dwells among us in the flesh.

"In many ways, this is the exact opposite message that modern man desperately craves. You see, when the Trinity said, "Let us make man in our image," He decided to create His own image bearer. We were supposed to be the temple of God where His Spirit would dwell, and we were to consciously return to His temple again and again. But we were not satisfied with being the image of God. We had to do things our way, we had to try and replace God. And now our efforts to become gods and make our own rules have left us fallen lower than the animals. We were supposed to rule this world, but now we are too self-destructive and rebellious to even govern ourselves.

"It never ceases to amaze me how badly people want to be animals. We want to simply pursue our desires, to do whatever feels good. But when we follow that instinct instead of the divine mandate woven deep into the fabric of our hearts to pursue something more, to bear the dignity reminiscent of God's temple, we descend into hell. At first, it starts with one obsession or another. Maybe it's an addiction to sex, or greed, or any number of other sins. And then those sins turn darker... even violent. And then we wind up bleeding and we can't figure out how we got there."

The boy's expression hadn't changed. He looked as lifeless as ever. Mo sighed as he planted his face in his hands. "This is so pointless! You can't hear a word I am saying and I keep talking." The defeated preacher slouched in his chair and leaned back. The Bible on his lap fell to the floor, but Mo did not bother to pick it up. Instead, Mo just sat there in an exasperated daze as sleep crept into his mind. But before his consciousness slipped the old man's eyes flew open as he sat up. "I'm so sorry. You don't have much time left. You could go at any moment, and here I am getting ready to fall asleep." Mo then halfheartedly laughed to himself. "Not that it matters."

The aging preacher had imagined the man at least waking and finding God before his final moment had passed. He had hoped that Paul's eyes would open and that the two would briefly discuss who is God. Then the man would die in peace, with a smile on his face, or even pull through and somehow live. Now that looked impossible, and Mo could feel the rising temptation to abandon hope. "Dear God, no one need know if this man heard a thing I said save him and you. But if it pleases you, will you give me a sign? Will you show me that there was still something left to preach to?" The old man noticed that his Bible had opened when it hit the floor. He picked the worn text off the cold tile and read the first verses he saw:

> And he that reapeth receiveth wages, and gathereth fruit unto life eternal: that both he that soweth and he that reapeth may rejoice together. And herein is that saying true, One soweth, and another reapeth.

Mo shook his head. "I am sorry. That was a selfish prayer. It does not matter whether or not I come to know his fate now. What matters is that he hears your voice. If it pleases you, give him one more chance to know you. Reach down into the depths of his heart and make him understand your name, let him yet bow the knee and call you Lord..."

In the midst of Mo's prayer, he did not recognize that the heart monitor was slowing, that the man's lifeline was fading faster. It was not until the dull buzzing of the machine produced a single, uninterrupted beep that Mo looked up with misty eyes and saw that Paul's body had finally given out for good.

"God, why did you bring me here? What was the point? Even if I had preached and no one had ever come to know the truth, at least they would have heard. I know your Word is life, but right now it just seems like I am surrounded by death." The preacher looked ragged and old. Great bags hung beneath his sunken eyes and his breathing strained against fatigue. Mo slowly rose and was about to leave when a thought ran through his mind. Mo approached the dead man lying in the hospital bed, leaned over, and whispered, "Now faith is the substance of things hoped for, the evidence of things not seen." Then Mo smiled and said, "see you in heaven."

.....

Several days later the preacher stood out on a busy street corner in the city's red light district. He had already seen hundreds of faces pass by that night. Each one of them lacked a care in the world. They wanted drugs and dance, not words and wisdom. But Mo remembered back to the last time he had considered leaving his ministry, to that poor boy with nothing to live for. The harvest was plentiful, but the workers were few. So the preacher dug down deep into his soul and told all passing by about the wellspring of life which could grow within them. And they mocked and scoffed the way they always did. But Mo did not tire. He knew that these people needed to know who God was, and that no one was beyond salvation.

Stephen DeRose

About the Author

Stephen DeRose holds a Bachelor's of Art in philosophy from the College of New Jersey as well as a Master's of Divinity from Westminster Theological Seminary, Philadelphia. He is a recipient of the Huff Science Scholarship, has presented at numerous conferences including an American Philosophical Association's annual meeting, and done graduate research at Saint Olaf College and Princeton Seminary. He previously worked as a Chaplin with the Navigators. He was also an Associate Pastor at the Highland Park Church of God in Gloucester City, New Jersey. He is currently a professional writer working on numerous projects related to education, economics, and philosophy. Many of his shorter education articles can be found on successfulstudent.org and thebestschools.org. He now lives with his wife Gina and his dog Blue in Iowa.